Cambridge Elements

Elements in Women Theatre Makers
edited by
Elaine Aston
Lancaster University
Melissa Sihra
Trinity College Dublin

CLEAN BREAK THEATRE COMPANY

Caoimhe McAvinchey
Queen Mary University of London

Sarah Bartley
Royal Central School of Speech and Drama

Deborah Dean
University of Warwick

Anne-marie Greene
University of York

Shaftesbury Road, Cambridge CB2 8EA, United Kingdom

One Liberty Plaza, 20th Floor, New York, NY 10006, USA

477 Williamstown Road, Port Melbourne, VIC 3207, Australia

314–321, 3rd Floor, Plot 3, Splendor Forum, Jasola District Centre, New Delhi – 110025, India

103 Penang Road, #05–06/07, Visioncrest Commercial, Singapore 238467

Cambridge University Press is part of Cambridge University Press & Assessment, a department of the University of Cambridge.

We share the University's mission to contribute to society through the pursuit of education, learning and research at the highest international levels of excellence.

www.cambridge.org
Information on this title: www.cambridge.org/9781009525893
DOI: 10.1017/9781009525909

© Caoimhe McAvinchey, Sarah Bartley, Deborah Dean and Anne-marie Greene 2024

This publication is in copyright. Subject to statutory exception and to the provisions of relevant collective licensing agreements, no reproduction of any part may take place without the written permission of Cambridge University Press & Assessment.

When citing this work, please include a reference to the DOI 10.1017/9781009525909

First published 2024

A catalogue record for this publication is available from the British Library.

ISBN 978-1-009-52589-3 Hardback
ISBN 978-1-009-52585-5 Paperback
ISSN 2634-2391 (online)
ISSN 2634-2383 (print)

Cambridge University Press & Assessment has no responsibility for the persistence or accuracy of URLs for external or third-party internet websites referred to in this publication and does not guarantee that any content on such websites is, or will remain, accurate or appropriate.

Clean Break Theatre Company

Elements in Women Theatre Makers

DOI: 10.1017/9781009525909
First published online: June 2024

Caoimhe McAvinchey
Queen Mary University of London

Sarah Bartley
Royal Central School of Speech and Drama

Deborah Dean
University of Warwick

Anne-marie Greene
University of York

Author for correspondence: Caoimhe McAvinchey, c.mcavinchey@qmul.ac.uk

Abstract: Clean Break is a women-only theatre company that grew out of a prisoner-led drama workshop that took place between 1977 and 1979 in HMP Askham Grange. In addition to its considerable impact on criminalised women and public understandings of the socio-political impact of their experiences, Clean Break has had a significant but under-acknowledged impact on contemporary British theatre. This Element examines three areas of Clean Break's theatre making history and organisational practices: its origin stories; its education and engagement work; and how the company's performance practices have, across five decades, adapted to directly intervene in carceral society. By highlighting Clean Break's distinct activist theatre making processes and practices, the Element makes explicit the genealogical connections of the company's past work and its impacts on contemporary feminist theatre practices.

Keywords: Clean Break, prison theatre, arts and criminal justice, feminist theatre, carceral society

© Caoimhe McAvinchey, Sarah Bartley, Deborah Dean and Anne-marie Greene 2024

ISBNs: 9781009525893 (HB), 9781009525855 (PB), 9781009525909 (OC)
ISSNs: 2634-2391 (online), 2634-2383 (print)

Contents

Introduction	1
1 Origin Stories	7
2 Education as a Practice of Endurance	24
3 Facts, Fictions and Narratives of Knowing in Carceral Society	46
Conclusion	65
References	67

Introduction

In August 1980, Clean Break Women Prisoners Theatre Company performed a double bill at the Pleasance Theatre, as part of the Edinburgh Festival Fringe. *In or Out,* set in HMP Holloway, was written and performed by Jenny Hicks and Eva Mottley; *Killers,* set in HMP Durham, was written and performed by Jacki Holborough with music by Cat Coull. The programme makes explicit that the company was 'formed by serving prisoners [...] and continued as a theatre workshop and touring group following the release of some of its members [...] The work emerges as a result of the varied experience of the authors and performers; IN OR OUT and KILLERS are examples of this experience' (Clean Break, 1980). The following quotation from *Killers* gives a sense not only of the company members' lived experience – the personal – but the ways in which Clean Break continually telescopes understanding from individual women's lives to its wider societal implications – the political. Their work addresses the criminalisation and punishment of women as the outcome of political decision-making processes about social control. It invites audiences to consider why society accepts that things are the way they are:

> How absurd it seems that we should be kept here like this. In separate little compartments, filed away – for three years ... or thirty. A matter of numbers. What you or anyone else is supposed to have done recedes into a dusty pile of papers that ceases to have meaning.
> Left only with isolated individuals coming together for group identification at times specified by system routine. You may mix together. You may not mix together. Two or three of you may mix in that corner, four or five of you in this space here. And the times and patterns at which this association may occur are worked out as carefully as an abstract painting – seeming haphazard but having, one suspects, all the skill of purposeful planning. (Holborough, 1980: 10)

After a successful run at the 1980 Edinburgh Festival Fringe, Clean Break toured the double bill to women's festivals, theatres, universities, prisons, hospitals and training conferences for prison psychologists and probation services. The collective of women had little formal training or funding but a strong sense of imperative, self-organisation and commitment to talk with audiences about women's experiences of incarceration and what they reveal of women's position in wider society: 'Women only spaces are really vital because if you are separated enough, if you take yourself out of this insidious patriarchy which you don't recognise when you are in it, you see it. It took me a long while to recognise what that word, [patriarchy], meant, and it was prison that did that for me' (Hicks, 2019).

Hicks's reflections on her experience of incarceration that fostered an understanding of the relationship between women's everyday experiences and the wider patriarchal systems they are enmeshed within, says something about the political moment and momentum that the company grew out of. Clean Break's imperative for action, to not only make visible and critique the systems and structures of patriarchal society through theatre, but to create alternative realities with it, is a collective political commitment: 'You just do it [...] You make connections, you enthuse people. You have to have something people are interested in' (Hicks, 2018).

More than forty years later, in the Spring of 2023, at the time of writing this Element, Clean Break Theatre Company continues to 'have something people are interested in'. The company is in rehearsals for *Dixon and Daughters,* a new play by Deborah Bruce, co-produced with and premiered at the National Theatre of Great Britain, London. Rehearsals are taking place both at the National Theatre and at Clean Break's purpose-built, women-only space in Kentish Town, North London. The all-women cast and crew include some who are Clean Break Members, women who are involved in the company's work that have lived experience of the criminal justice system or are at risk of entering it. The playwright, Deborah Bruce, has been a Clean Break Writer in Residence (2016–18), immersed in the life and work of the company: she ran writing workshops in prisons, developed a writers' circle with Members and wrote a short play, *Hear* (2016), informed by the voices and insights of women serving prison sentences and the impact these had after their release. *Hear* was performed by Clean Break Members at the House of Lords and the Ministry of Justice for politicians, civil servants, and criminal justice staff. Concurrent with *Dixon and Daughters*, Clean Break is in the middle of a UK tour of Sonia Jalaly's *Catch* (2023), a short educational play and accompanying workshop about the vital role of women's centres in supporting marginalised and dispossessed women in the UK. Staged in a range of different contexts (universities, probation services, community centres, conferences), *Catch* is performed by a cast of Clean Break Members.

Over the past five decades, Clean Break has evolved from a small cooperative into an internationally recognised theatre and advocacy organisation that places stories of women, crime, and punishment centre stage. During this time, Clean Break has commissioned over 100 original plays which expose women's experiences of structural inequality and violence through criminalisation and incarceration. From its inception, the company has been committed to performing work in a broad range of venues to reach as many different audiences as possible: from theatre spaces such as the Royal Court, The Crucible, Theatre Clywd and Chichester Theatre, to non-theatre sites and events, such as mental health conferences and women's prisons. Simultaneously, off-stage, in the company's women-only centre, Members can currently access a range of creative skills provision (and previously could participate in an education and training programme) that address the inequities facing women with experience of the criminal justice system. From the outset, the company had an elastic and accommodating sense of what this means: 'Clean Break is not just open to women prisoners and ex-prisoners, but also to any woman who has had experience of confinement or the criminal justice system (i.e. a drug rehabilitation or youth custody centre or even a police cell)' (Clean Break, 1989). Members[1] are offered training, personal and professional development, and opportunities to connect with a network of voluntary sector services, higher education, professional arts opportunities, and employment. Travel, food, and support with childcare ensure that the every-day structural barriers to participation are acknowledged and addressed.

Internationally, there are some theatre companies dedicated to working with women with prison experience such as the Medea Project (USA), Somebody's Daughter (Australia) and Teatro Yeses (Spain) and increasingly there is documentation and research available about the work of specific theatre programmes with incarcerated women, which detail the nuanced particularity of their lives as well as different approaches to theatre making in different cultural contexts (McAvinchey, 2020). Clean Break's evolution and longevity, as well as the diversity of its practices over its existence (commissioning and producing new plays for a wide range of audiences; its advocacy and leadership in both the criminal justice system and theatre industry, and it history of delivering a responsive education and training programme – which ran from the 1990s until 2016), mean that it is unique within a wider set of theatre practices with and about criminalised women. Aspects of the company's work have been the subject of academic research, mainly in theatre and performance (Bartley, 2019, 2021, 2022; McAvinchey, 2020 a, b, c, d; McPhee, 2019, 2020; Walsh, 2012, 2014, 2016, 2019) and criminology (Merrill and Frigon, 2015) and there have been evaluations surveying the company's economic and cultural impact (NCP, 2011; Busby and Abraham, 2015). This is the first extended scholarly study to focus solely on the work of the company. The research which underpins it is interdisciplinary, informed by the *Women/Theatre/Justice* research project, undertaken by scholars in theatre and performance, and work and industrial relations.[2] Whilst there are many possible books that could be written about Clean

---

[1] Throughout the company's history, women with direct experience of the justice system have been variously referred to as the Theatre Workshop, Students, or Members. In the Element, we name them according to the term used during the period in the company's history that we are addressing.

[2] Women/Theatre/Justice is the umbrella title for research and public engagement activities that are part of Clean Break: Women, Theatre, Organisation and the Criminal Justice System (2019–21).

Break, due to this research project's unique interdisciplinary approach, we examine Clean Break projects and performances – on stage, in prisons, and at their base – as well as the work of *making* these projects. We draw on performance analysis, interviews, and an in-depth engagement with playscripts, education portfolios, and operational documentation held in the company's archive. As is frequently the case with arts organisations delivering projects in and around the criminal justice system, these histories are – at times – partial and obscured due to the opacity of the criminal justice system and any activities which happen within its parameters. As such, we draw together multiple narratives, documentary fragments, and playtexts to illuminate the range of creative projects and working practices at play over the five decades of the company's work. In this Element, we have chosen to foreground three areas of Clean Break: its origin stories; its education and engagement work; and how its practices have, across five decades, 'then' and 'now', adapted to directly intervene in carceral society. Before we attend to each of these areas, we need to introduce the contexts that Clean Break has navigated and evolved through.

Women and Carceral Society

Vivien Stern articulates the ubiquity of prisons: 'Everyone has them. It is as normal to have prisons as to have schools or hospitals' (1998: xx). However, despite the growth in the international prison population – the latest figures from the World Prison Population List (2021) report over 11.5 million incarcerated people – people's access to prison and their knowledge about it is largely mediated and shaped through cultural representation rather than personal experience: news and documentary footage; memoirs and novels; television and film ensuring that the symbolic power of prison has become 'as much a basic metaphor of our cultural imagination as it is of our penal policy' (Garland, 1990: 260).

Whilst the definition of carceral relates to, or of, prison, carceral geography makes explicit the myriad ways in which prison – as penal policy, site and metaphor – seeps across a material perimeter to produce disciplinary techniques which shape subjects beyond it (Moran, 2018; Routley, 2017). A carceral society is one where the carceral 'reaches all the disciplinary mechanisms that function throughout society' (Foucault, 1977:298), rippling from the prison to the social body as a whole (Moran, Turner and Schliehe, 2018: 669). For example, a prison sentence may be time- and place-specific; however, the

---

This interdisciplinary Arts and Humanities Research Council (AHRC) funded project is led by the authors of this book, academics in theatre and performance studies and work and employment relations, in partnership with Clean Break theatre company. You can learn more about the research project here: https://womentheatrejustice.org/

shame and stigma attached to it endure long after a sentence has been served. Carceral geography's examination of 'who and where is governed through carceral logics and the precise forms that these take, as well as the subjectivities produced through these processes' (Routley, 2017) informs our consideration of Clean Break's practices as a critique of and resistance to carceral society and penal spectatorship (Brown, 2009, 2013).

Further, despite the many cultural variations in the development of prisons across the globe, there is one constant: men have always been the majority. Currently, women make up 6 per cent of the global prison population (PRI, 2021). Research into the experience of women in the criminal justice system from law, feminist criminology and prison studies confirms that, as a direct consequence, women are marginalised because of their gender, because they have been criminalised and because they are the minority (Agozino, 1997; McIvor, 2004; Sharpe, 2012). This lack of consideration of women's specific needs is summarised by Ramsbotham during his tenure as Her Majesty's Chief Inspector of Prisons (1995–2001), 'It is not merely a question of women receiving equal treatment to men; in the prison system equality is everywhere conflated with uniformity; women are treated as if they are men' (1997: para. 3.46). This failure to recognise the need for different approaches is evidenced in ideologies that inform the language of the law (Kennedy, 1993, 2018), the architectural design and material conditions of women's prisons (Moore and Scranton, 2014) and the endemic political inertia that impedes penal reform attending to the needs of women, communities, and society (Corston, 2007; McCorkel, 2013). The feminisation of poverty (Bradshaw, 2002), the elision between welfare policy and penal policy and racism (Wacquant, 2011) means that women are particularly vulnerable to political forces of regulation and punishment.

The particularity of women's experiences is detailed in Clean Break's rich repertoire of plays. The following offers an introductory snapshot of the range and nuance of this work. Paulette Randall's *24%* (1991) examines the systemic racism that shapes the lives of young Black women, within and beyond the criminal justice system; the issues faced by characters navigating complex mental health needs in a system that fails to address them is dramatised in Sarah Daniels' *Head-rot Holiday* (1993), set in a special secure hospital, and echoed twenty years later in Vivienne Franzmann's *Sounds like an Insult* (2015). *Mules* (1996) by Winsome Pinnock traced the drug trafficking routes between the UK and Jamaica, exposing a system that pushes the most excluded women to try and find a way out of poverty. A decade later, Lucy Kirkwood's, *it felt empty when the heart went at first but it's alright now* (2009), invited audiences to think about the implications of sex-trafficking when they witnessed

Dijana, a young Croatian woman, trapped by debt, grief and, despite all the evidence to the contrary, hope for an alternative life. *Joanne* (2015), by Deborah Bruce, Theresa Ikoko, Laura Lomas, Chino Odimba and Ursula Rani Sarma, is a play that captures the multifaceted landscapes Clean Break addresses by staging the final twenty-four hours in the life of a young woman after she is released from prison. We never meet the eponymous Joanne, but aspects of her life are revealed through the testimony of five women, played by the same actor (Tanya Moodie in the original production). Each of these five characters has a role to play in organisations and institutions that Joanne comes into contact with before and after prison: school, the police, the NHS, a charity that supports prisoners as they prepare for release and a hostel which provides accommodation for homeless prisoners. *Joanne* exemplifies Clean Break's commitment to nurturing state-of-the-nation plays that depict the lasting impact of the societal and political neglect of women who come into contact with the criminal justice system. In brief, Clean Break's plays disturb and disrupt assumptions about women, crime, punishment and justice, inviting audiences to be aware of and take responsibility for the narratives they witness, perpetuate or question.

In Section 1, we interrogate the origin story of Clean Break, focusing on the narrative of two women founders within its collective beginnings, to reflect on how this story has been told at various times in the company's history and to what ends. We consider the ways in which the company positioned itself in relation to wider contemporary practices, especially feminist theatre and the women's theatre movement of the late 1970s and 1980s, and assert that the alternative theatre movement is an under-acknowledged antecedent of what we now refer to as prison theatre and socially engaged theatre. Rather than consider Clean Break being founded in one moment by two people, we come to think about founding as an iterative process over time.

In Section 2, we review these wider structures and processes within Clean Break's education and engagement activities, identifying the personal and political work courses offered. We assert how education functions as a practice of endurance across the company's work; paying particular attention to the longevity of Clean Break and the role of education in its work supporting women who encounter the structural violence of the criminal justice system. We identify how the company has endured in the face of an increasingly hostile landscape and persistently fought to maintain a space in which criminalised women can access agency and creative imagination. We map how the company adapted in the light of government policy, funding, and organisational changes to consider how Clean Break has secured both a site (a purpose-built organisational home) and developed models of organisational practice which promote endurance.

In Section 3, we consider how Clean Break, through its varied theatre practices, disrupts an understanding of the social and political power relations that impact women, crime, and justice. We draw on Clean Break productions and archival materials from across five decades (*Killers, Decade, Inside Bitch* and *[BLANK]*) and engage with Pat Carlen's ideas of the 'criminological imagination' (1983, 2019) and ideas of social epistemology (Brady and Fricker, 2016; Fricker et al., 2016) and epistemic injustice (Fricker, 2007, 2016) to consider some of the ways that Clean Break's attention to women's experiences of criminalisation develops new understandings about prison as a fabrication of social control and power relations in carceral society. We argue that Clean Break's work is an act of feminist social epistemology, with theatre practices expanding audiences' 'knowledge, information, belief and judgement' (Fricker et al., 2019: xvii) about women and criminalisation.

Our access to cultural narratives about women within the criminal justice system, particularly through television and film, gives us the impression that we know something about their lives and experiences. Fictional narratives featuring women in police custody, court and prisons are readily available on our screens and in our mind's eye. Criminologists, particularly popular criminologists, evidence the power of cultural representations as systems of knowledge circulation in generating public knowledge about crime, criminals and punishment (Rafter and Brown, 2011). However, popular criminology has not engaged with theatre as a system of knowledge generation. Across this Element, we consider how Clean Break's work contributes to a popular criminological understanding about prison and women's experiences of it – prison not only as a site but also as an idea which, literally, is a fabrication of power relations in carceral society.

For more than forty years Clean Break has survived seismic shifts in Britain's social, cultural, political and economic landscape to create structures and practices that have had a significant impact for criminalised women and public understandings of the sociopolitical impact of their experiences. This Element examines Clean Break theatre company's origins and practices to consider not only *what* Clean Break does but *how* it does it.

1 Origin Stories

The longevity of Clean Break Theatre Company and the fluidity of its organisational structures and approaches over time enable its work to be situated across distinctive and overlapping practices including the alternative theatre movement, community arts, arts and criminal justice, applied theatre, socially engaged arts, new writing and contemporary British theatre. A consideration of the company's history illuminates both shifts and intersections in its own practices as well as these artistic lineages. Here we interrogate the 'origin story' of Clean Break to investigate how the company's narrative has been deployed, occluded and entrenched at different times in its history. Specifically, we reflect on how Clean Break has articulated its founding years at different times to consider and problematise the ways theatre histories are shaped by the priorities of contemporary cultural landscapes. Further, in attending to this organisation's origin story, we seek to expand understandings of what it is to found a socially committed theatre company at a particular political and cultural moment and assert that the alternative theatre movement is an under-acknowledged antecedent of both applied theatre and arts in the criminal justice system.

1.1 An Alternative History

The 1968 Theatres Act abolished censorship of the theatre; the Lord Chamberlain's role, which, since 1737, had been to decide what was and wasn't fit to be licensed and seen by the public, was made redundant. Prior to this, theatre was dominated by practices that generated and maintained hierarchical structures in the creation, production and management of work. Capitalist models ensured a pyramid of power where a small number of people made decisions about what narratives and lives were represented and those that were not; about who was employed and who was not. The authority of the writer and director was privileged (Rebellato, 1999, 2013; Shellard, 1999). There was a robust economy of building-based companies such as the Royal National Theatre, Royal Shakespeare Company, and West End theatres staging large-scale productions with 'networks of provincial and repertory theatres, which were complemented by a number of "Little Theatres" or "arts theatres"' (Jones, 2021: 1).

However, with the abolition of censorship came the rise of alternative, political theatre, with its outcrop of countercultural companies that flourished throughout the 1970s (Craig, 1980; DiCenzo, 1996; Itzin, 1983). Alternative theatre groups upended assumptions about the role of theatre in society; about which stories, subjects, and lives were deemed important to represent; about who got to make work; and the means by which the work was made. Maria DiCenzo warns against, 'lumping together all left-sounding theatre groups, into one broad continuum, [as it] submerges critical political differences in the name of unity' (1996: 18). Although it is important to recognise the very different political ambitions of the companies that evolved during this time, there are some shared characteristics that connect them – characteristics relevant to Clean Break in its formative years. These include how the work was predominantly small-scale and made by companies explicit about the politics that shaped their theatre (e.g. Gay Sweatshop, Welfare State, Theatre of Black Women). Another common feature related to the way in which not all company members had training or experience in theatre, but all were committed to the possibility of social and political change through it. The themes of the work reflected the sociopolitical concerns of the group. For example, Black Theatre Co-operative portrayed life from a Black perspective in the UK (Goddard, 2002) and Inter-Action created an eclectic and responsive range of arts interventions in the lives of communities (Itzin, 1983). Many of the companies modelled collective decision-making and shared responsibility in the devising, writing, and producing of work; rather than assuming that audiences would come to designated theatre buildings, there was a commitment by companies to take the work to where people already gathered – in community and educational spaces in rural as well as urban environments.

For many alternative-theatre companies post-show discussions, often in the venue's foyer or bar rather than onstage, were a key strategy in audience engagement to increase awareness of the specific challenges faced, and political advocacy for the communities they represented. Post-show conversations were an integral part of Clean Break's practice:

> We always had, if we could, a discussion session after every play. That was the whole point of it really, to open up the dialogue with our audiences, that's part of the drive from the beginning really, to say 'here we are, let's talk about this. Let's not hide it.' It wasn't always easy, but audiences were great, usually. They were really, usually quite interested and enthusiastic about us.
> (Hicks and Holborough, 2020)

In an interview in 1979, company member Sasha Hutchinson noted the significance of the post-show conversation for the company: 'They usually get round to asking us what we did and what prison was like. Then they discover that we aren't a different species' (Harker, 1979). Similarly, these post-show discussions also provided spaces for women to build connections, with members of the audience frequently standing up and declaring their own experiences with the criminal justice system. The post-show moment was a significant part of the theatre event, an opportunity to deepen understanding of the experiences of incarcerated women involved in the performance and advocate further for the political mission of the company to improve public understanding of criminalised women.

In brief, these alternative, collective and collaborative modes of theatre making, in principle if not always in practice, were bound up with the political and aesthetic agendas of theatre companies. Whilst most of the companies

Figure 1 Clean Break Women's Theatre Company Image (1980)

detailed in Itzin's extraordinary *British Alternative Theatre Directory of Playwrights, Directors and Designers* (1983) are no longer in operation, there are many artists and a small number of companies, including Clean Break, who were part of this movement that continue to make explicitly political, socially engaged and applied performances in the early twenty-first century.

That Clean Break emerged as part of the UK's alternative theatre movement is an 'origin story' overlooked by alternative-theatre histories. Equally, Clean Break's relationship to alternative theatre and histories of collective modes of creation has not been particularly present in the company's own discussion of its practice. Furthermore, an elision of Clean Break's alternative history has occurred through the more recent attention given to the company's strand of education work and the way in which Clean Break has come to articulate the benefits of this with reference to social inclusion and criminal justice outcomes (see Section 2). Hence, it is not surprising to find that the company is now primarily considered in the context of applied and social theatre. Today, on UK Drama degrees, at undergraduate and master's level, Clean Break receives most attention through the lens of applied theatre scholarship which is a referent for UK applied theatre practice. But to recollect Clean Break's early years as a group of non-hierarchical, collaborative theatre makers, is to recognise the relationship of applied performance to a radical genealogy of performance making, thereby challenging understandings of UK applied performance genealogies as predominantly associated with the government emphasis on social inclusion in the

1990s, which sought to deploy culture to change the behaviour of marginalised or excluded individuals through arts interventions.[3] In short, to recognise how Clean Break was more embedded in circuits of alternative theatre, performing at The Drill Hall Arts Centre and The Women's Arts Alliance Women's Festival and sharing stages with companies such as Split Britches, Gay Sweatshop, Spiderwoman, and Sadista Sisters, is to reaffirm their genealogical connections to an alternative theatre history.

1.1.1 Clean Break and Feminism

Such a history also has to take account of Clean Break as a women's theatre group. With a mission to advocate for a better awareness of criminalised women, Clean Break appears to align with the women's theatre movement of the 1970s and 1980s. On and off the stage, the 1970s was the decade of second-wave feminism. The climate of feminist activism saw significant advances for women: the British Women's Liberation Movement was founded in 1970; in 1972 the first issues of the feminist magazine *Spare Rib* and the Marxist-feminist magazine, *Red Rag* were published; The Almost Free Theatre hosted the first Women's Theatre Festival in 1973; The National Women's Aid Federation was formed in 1974 providing support and refuge for women and children experiencing domestic violence; key legislation including the Sex Discrimination Act and the Employment Protection Act were introduced in 1975; the first Reclaim the Night march in Britain was held in Edinburgh in 1977; and the Southall Black Sisters was formed in 1979. The decade was bookended by women-led strikes and protest movements, with the Dagenham machinists at the Ford factory striking over equal pay in 1968, the Greenham Common Peace Camp set up in 1981, and Women Against Pit Closures established in 1984. This surge of collective action was mirrored in theatre with the rise of women's groups including Theatre of Black Women, Beryl and the Perils, Bloomers, Cunning Stunts, Monstrous Regiment, Sadista Sisters and the Women's Theatre Group. As Graham Saunders argued 'If a golden age could ever said to have existed for women's theatre companies, it would be the ten-year span between 1975 and 1985' (2015: 64).[4]

---

[3] This is not to say that Clean Break's work during a period in which government policy prioritised inclusion was not significant and indeed deeply meaningful for the Members, artists, and educators involved. Rather, recognising the wider lineages of the company serves to illuminate the breadth, diversity, and political complexity of Clean Break over five decades.

[4] Lizabeth Goodman (1993), Elaine Aston (1995, 2003) and Michelene Wandor (1984, 1986) examine the sociopolitical contexts that shaped the conditions of women making theatre at this time.

However, since its founding, the identity of Clean Break as a feminist organisation has been continually contested by some company members and observers. In those early years, this contestation reflected divisions within the feminist movement that centred on staging violence against women. In a 1980 show report, theatre academic Jill Davis noted in an Arts Council Drama Panel:

> What really turned me off, though, was [...] the very high level of verbal and physical violence in the piece. The rest of the audience at Action Space (mostly women, mostly feminists, a lot of gays) were visibly disturbed too. Several women left. There was a sense in the audience that the first rule of feminist ethics has been broken – sisters don't hit sisters, not even in plays, unless they have good reason, unless something is being demonstrated by it. And the violence in this show seemed completely gratuitous. Very nasty. (qtd in Saunders, 2015: 19)

There was an undeniable violence to early plays such as *A Question of Habit* (1979), in which an inexperienced terrorist kills a nun; *Under Eros* (1979), which depicts a mother walking her 'uncontrollable' daughter through Piccadilly on a dog lead; and *In Or Out* (1980), which stages the encounters of two women, a prison officer and a woman about to be released, depicting the acute oppressions of the justice system. Hicks and Holborough reflect on the company's turbulent relationship with some feminist audiences and theatre makers at that time:

> Hicks: Well, our first brush with feminism ... [laughs]
> Holborough: Oh, it didn't go well.
> Hicks: [...] Jacki wrote this very irreverent play, called *A Question of Habit* where she has women torturing other women. [...]
> Holborough: It was my humour. It was about women terrorists in a Bayswater basement [...] it's all part of initiation for a new young recruit, they're going to pretend to torture this nun. And it goes terribly wrong and the young recruit kills the nun. But the women's audience at the Women's Alliance, they did not like that. They didn't like any aspect of women being violent to anyone.
> Hicks: We were heavily criticised by the feminists, except for Gay Sweatshop women, who we were always friends with and they were fun, and just as irreverent. And true to themselves.
> Holborough: They did understand that –
> Hicks: That there might be blood on the carpet.
> Holborough: There might be blood, there very often was with them. And with us occasionally. (Hicks and Holborough, 2020)

That there would be 'blood on the carpet' has been important to Clean Break across their body of work. The criminal justice system they depict is violent and often the women who end up embroiled within that system have encountered violence; almost two thirds of women in prison in 2022 are survivors of domestic abuse. In the 1970s and now, the company's advocacy mission means their work can often be 'disturbing' as Davis notes, but it seeks to disturb and disrupt in order to bring increased action and attention towards the criminalisation of women and desperate need for reformation within the criminal justice system.

Locating Clean Break's emergence within the alternative theatre movement and unpicking the complexities of their identity as a women's theatre company at this time, importantly expands our understanding of how the company continues to utilise political theatre to advocate for women with lived experience of the criminal justice system and underscores the contentious framing of their work as feminist. While categorisation as a feminist company has never been claimed, Clean Break can be argued as such, notably, for example, in its fulfilment of the criteria in Patricia Yancey Martin's (1990) taxonomy of what comprises a feminist organisation. Martin establishes ten dimensions: ideology, values, goals, outcomes, founding circumstances, structure, practices, members and membership, scope and scale, external relations. From the perspective of this analytical framework, Clean Break meets and has always met, the criteria for a feminist organisation. In the phrase used since 2018 in the company's revised business model, this has put 'women at the heart' of strategy and practice. The company was created to serve women, to advocate for their specific needs within the criminal justice system, and it continues to centre their stories onstage, while hoping to position women with lived experience more consistently in the structure and decision-making practices of the organisation and the theatre sector more broadly. While particular strands, waves or iterations of feminism might be at odds with Clean Break – and indeed some Members and Artists involved in the company might resist the categorisation – it sits within Martin's conceptualisation of feminism.

1.2 Complicating the Origin Story

Beyond locating the organisation's historical lineage within broader artistic and social movements, we are also interested in understanding the internal organisation of the company in its early years. Clean Break Theatre Company's origin narrative, articulated across all areas of its current artistic, educational and advocacy work, and reiterated in scholarship, identifies 'two women' as the founders of the company (some indicative examples of this narrative appear in

Devlin, 1998: 343; Goodman, 1993: 205; Gupta, 2002: n.p). This narrative is reiterated in the company's current website in the 'About Us' section: 'Clean Break was founded by two women in prison who believed in the power of theatre to transform lives' (Clean Break, n.d).

Conversely, some of the company's promotional materials from their first decade complicate this 'two women' founder narrative by articulating the emergence of the company as a collective of women, also often referring to them as a drama workshop. For example, the *Avenues* programme states: 'Clean Break is a dynamic and truly unique women's theatre company, founded in Askham Grange Prison by serving prisoners in 1978 and continued as a workshop and touring company of women ex-prisoners since 1979' (Clean Break, 1982).

The collective approach of the group is further affirmed by Hicks and Holborough in their early letters to Susan McCormick, the governor of HMP Askham Grange, who became a friend, advocate and, arguably, a producer for the company: 'On reading the *Guardian* article [you sent to us] I was struck by the refence to lacking discipline in many women's groups: being terribly indulgent with each other and letting everyone do their bit, which is exactly how we work' (Holborough to McCormick, 1979b).

This disjuncture between the entrenched narrative of Clean Break emerging from the work of two women, who are at various points anonymised or named as Hicks and Holborough, and the pairs' own articulation of the collective endeavour of its early years, prompts a reconsideration of the role of the founder, the timeframe for founding and a reorientation of Clean Break's history as part of a movement of collective theatre-making practices.

It was in 1977 that Jenny Hicks and Jacki Holborough first met at 'H'-Wing – a high-security unit for women within Durham Prison, a site that housed incarcerated men. In an interview, Holborough recalled their first meeting:

> After we'd met in the exercise yard, Jenny Hicks said to me, "You're the actress, aren't you? We heard about you on the radio, we knew you were coming here. [...] "Wouldn't this be a great place to have theatre". And the exercise yard at Durham is like a wire ... no nature at all there, not even a blade of grass. [...] So I said, 'Yeah, it would be great for something like *The Trojan Women*, thinking [I was being] very clever, and Jenny knew *The Trojan Women*, we laughed. And from then we started playing with the idea of having some theatre in this bleak exercise yard. (Hicks and Holborough, 2020)

There followed some tentative efforts to create a performance, notably Holborough recounts a group of women gathering regularly to sing along to a *Jesus Christ Superstar* cassette tape with the hopes of performing the show in the yard, but staff at Durham Prison soon shut this down as a security risk (ibid).

It was when Hicks and Holborough met again later at HMP Askham Grange, an open security prison in North Yorkshire, that Clean Break mark their formation. The prison already ran an annual Christmas pantomime performed by incarcerated women (with regular guest appearances from prison staff and the local vicar) for an invited audience, including locals from the villages of Askham Bryan and Askham Richard (*Yorkshire Evening Post*, 1978). In 1978 the pantomime *Goody Two Shoes*, was performed by a cast of forty women including Hicks and Holborough. At the start of 1979, several of the women involved in the performance approached Susan McCormick, Askham Grange's Governor, to ask for permission to continue a regular theatre workshop after the pantomime finished. McCormick encouraged the women's ambition with around twenty of them attending weekly theatre sessions to explore different playtexts (by Joe Orton, Spike Milligan, and Agatha Christie) and ultimately write their own work (Hicks and Holborough, 2020). Holborough notes, 'what started off as a bit of fun and defiance of the system became something much more radical and personal when the women decided to write their own material: material that was "something about us"' (Hicks and Holborough, 2018). The theatre workshop became a space for shared devising and co-creation.

With the support of McCormick, the group, while still incarcerated, staged *Efemera* at York Arts Centre in 1978, under the company name ASK'EM OUT. *Efemera* exemplifies the company's collective beginnings – its six acts of varying lengths devised and performed by twenty-one women involved in the prison's theatre workshop. There was also a strong musical component to the show with nine songs and four musicians involved. Ros Davies, the music teacher at HMP Askham Grange, was a key ally and collaborator. The series of scenes and songs was held together through the framework of a newspaper room and a sharing of stories. This two-hour production was the first performance staged outside of prison by a group of incarcerated people in Britain.

While the women were given special dispensation to leave the prison in the evening to do the two shows, the Home Office required that the performances were not advertised as created and performed by women serving prison sentences. Instead, the freesheet for the performance reads: 'ASK'EM OUT is an ad hoc group of women from a wide variety of social backgrounds, never to be together again, and local only for a short time' (*Efemera*, 1978). The listed cast names also offered a tongue-in-cheek indication of the company's history, including Miss de Meanour and Miss Phitt. Indeed, there was an appetite and interest from the public to understand what women in prison

J. HOLBOROUGH

```
GOODRICKE G/169   FRIDAY OCTOBER 27 - THIS FRIDAY - 8.00 GOODRICKE G/169
                        'EFEMERA' by ASK'EM OUT
ASK'EM OUT is an ad hoc group of women from a wide variety of social backgrounds,
never to be together again, and local only for a short time.

EFEMERA is a group of scenes conceived and composed by members of the group, and
originally set in a newspaper office. What's this about a newspaper office?
There's not a newspaper in sight! Never believe what you read ................

Scene I:    ROSA'S SOHO DRINKING CLUB (perhaps)
                Issy, the barmaid         - Lorraine Quiche
                Rosa herself              - Dora Knocker
                Clara, a psychiatrist     - Abery Stwyth
                Entertainer               - Moron Telly
                Waitress                  - Amanda Lynn
                Fiona, an heiress         - Martina Bianca
                Shirley, an ex-con        - A. Borealis
                Silent Drinker            - Dusty Rhodes
                Samantha Detroit          - Crystal Chandelier

Scene II:   AIRPORT '78 (with a bit of luck)
                Reporter                  - Aurora B.
                Abi                       - Dolly Tubb
                Cass                      - Miss de Meanour
                Air Hostess               - Angel Delight

Scene III:  STUDIO SEEN  (if the actors are drunk enough)
                Voice over                - Crystal Chandelier
                Busy Lizzie               - Miss de Meaner
                Cactus/Mrs. Murdoch       - Viola Ence/Angel Delight
                Rubber Plant              - Abery Stwyth
                Begonia                   - Marsha Mallow
                Ice Plant                 - Miss Phitt
                Basil                     - Dolly Tubb
                Florrie                   - Che de Laine

Scene IV:   UNDER EROS (Action-packed)
                Policeman                 - Dusty Rhodes/Drew Bludd
                Eros                      - Dusty Rhodes
                Busker                    - Moron Telly
                Maggie                    - Martina Bianca
                November                  - Crystal Chandelier

Scene V:    UNDER EROS (Mercifully short)
                Mrs. A.                   - Miss Phitt
                Mrs. B.                   - Dora Knocker
                Jasmine                   - Lorraine Quiche

Scene VI:   IN A BAYSWATER BASEMENT (not for those of a nervous disposition -
                                                     sex and violence)
                Ingrid                    - Crystal Chandelier
                Antonia                   - Aurora Borealis
                Ariel                     - Moron Telly
                Margaret                  - Dolly Tubb
                Phyllis                   - Martina Bianca

Cleaning Ladies - Vi O'Lett, Drew Bludd.       Lighting - Flo Ressant
Cut-outs, push-ons, pop-ups, fly-ins and drop-outs - Dusty Rhodes
Costumes - Marsha Mallow, Che de Laine, Miss Phitt
Wigs     - Miss Phitt
Musicians - Amanda Lynn, Aurora, Moron Telly, Abery Stwyth
Songs:   Early Autumn, Burns/Herman;  And then he hit me, Stepney Sisters;
         No no not tonight, Ms. Telly's 4th-year girls;  Cast-Iron Sue, Hazel;
         Picking, Irene;  Caught you in a lie, Louisa Marks;  Knocking on Heaven's Door
         B. Dylan;  Silver Threads Among the Gold;  Symphony of Violence, Baez.

Thanks to Bernard Harris for arranging things.
```

Figure 2 *Efemera* (1978) Company Programme

had to say. As Holborough recalls, the mandate from the Home Office did not hold for long:

> We were going to have a real outside audience who weren't supposed to know we were prisoners, but of course word had got around. The York Arts Centre was absolutely packed. [...] Some of the women had never been in a theatre, never seen a theatre, you know. We were a very, very diverse group and

> I thought, will it all hold together? And it held together so brilliantly. [...] I thought, it works, we can do this [...]. It was really moving and I just always remember that night, that first night in York, I thought oh, we can be in the theatre, we can be this thing, a women prisoners' theatre company. (Hicks and Holborough, 2020)

Holborough's reflection on the first public performance by the women who would later become Clean Break, affirms the collective emergence of the company. She speaks to the 'we', the group, and the realisation of this brilliant thing: 'a women prisoners' theatre company'.

This opaque introduction of the company to the public underscores the complexities around visibility that are enmeshed in Clean Break's work. As previously noted, identity politics played a crucial role in the formation of many alternative companies. In the case of Clean Break, women were making visible their experience with the criminal justice system, which at this point in the company's history generally meant women had lived experience of the system. In many ways, founding also lies in a naming and a willingness to be named as a founder of a women prisoners' theatre company. Indeed, at different points in the company's history the naming of Hicks and Holborough as the two founders has changed. Throughout the 1990s and 2000s in company narratives and wider scholarship the pair were only referred to as 'two women in prison'. We propose this is due to a mixture of factors: the pair undertaking other professional endeavours and a desire for their position as founders not to tie Clean Break to one idea of what it could be. But during the company's first decade in existence, Hicks and Holborough stood firmly as Clean Break Women and continued to make themselves visible to funders, arts organisations, press, and audiences in order to engage wider publics in their work.

Following the production of *Efemera*, a letter from Jenny and Jacki to Susan, with a capitalised 'CLEAN-BREAK WOMENS THEATRE COMPANY' at the top of the page, moves beyond imagining the possibility of a theatre company made up of prison experienced women, it is a declaration that it already exists:

> Dear Governor,
> We are in the process of forming the drama workshop we discussed with you last year.
> We are working on the material which will need to be rehearsed (in order to convince people to give us their stage!)
> To do this it is necessary to contact members of the group who are still in prison. Would it be possible therefore for us to write to Krissy Stephens and Adrienne Macleod?

It would be very helpful for the future if you could put in contact with us any likely new members who may be interested in joining the workshop. With thanks for all the help and encouragement you've given us.

Sincerely,
Jenny Hicks
Jacki Holborough. (Hicks and Holborough, 1979)

This letter is the first formal articulation of the company that would become Clean Break. It illustrates the clarity of the company's desire to 'be together again' and Susan McCormick's unacknowledged role as the first producer of the company. By facilitating the communication between women still serving sentences and those who had been released, McCormick collaborated with Clean Break in its transition from a prison drama workshop to a theatre company that, months later, was presenting work at the Women's Arts Alliance Festival and Edinburgh Fringe.

Clean Break began as a collective, or co-operative, whereas now it is organised into departments with section heads, reporting lines and a senior leadership team. Yet, in the face of successive waves of personnel changes and business models, Clean Break has retained a continuity in terms of its objectives and spirit. The contemporary company, working in a transformed political, technological and funding landscape, can be understood as not only connected to, but also as the *result* of, its original incarnation. This point is made more specifically by Zerubavel (1993: 458), who states that: 'Examining the way groups construct their beginnings is . . . indispensable to any study of the development of collective identity'. Further, as Godard (2013) emphasises, institutional norms have deep roots in particular historical conditions. These norms are 'cognitively embedded in the way actors think about institutions, and are structurally embedded in the design of institutions and the distribution of power resources', resulting in, as Thelen (2010) has argued, the 'constraints and opportunities' within which choices are made. It is arguable that the origin story of Clean Break has been mobilised both externally and internally: the two women's experience speaking to a transformational power of arts practice in carceral environments and the emergence of the company from women with lived experience maintaining a level of legitimacy. We see this framing of the origin narrative as key to enabling disparate personalities to work through the everyday challenges of maintaining a successful organisation. No matter what the profile of the two founders has been in terms of Clean Break's 'origin story' for both internal and external audiences, the shared, collective dimensions of the early years seem to still animate and inform decision-making in the company today which is unusually collaborative for a hierarchical organisation. A path was set, one shaped by the alternative theatre movement and by women's politicised understanding of their place in society during the 1970s.

1.3 Founding as an Iterative Process

Maria DiCenzo asserts that the collective structures of alternative-theatre companies were an attempt to democratise production processes and reflect a wider politics of equality that many companies were thematically addressing in their work. While both Hicks and Holborough were keen to assert the significance of collaboration in the early years of the company, they did note their own individual commitments to administrative, fundraising and producing tasks, to continue developing the company:

> Jenny and I are carrying the whole weight of the organisation thus far: in fact we didn't know whether or not we were even going to manage to get a group together at first but now it looks like we're going to have more interested people than we could hope for. (Holborough to McCormick, 1979a)

> The group is now a co-operative with rules and bank account. Very basic rules and very basic bank account – but it's a beginning. Rowntree's are sending us a cheque for £150 through Women's Research and Resources Centre (a charitable body) and the Nancy Balfour Trust sent a cheque for £100 directly to the group. We're waiting to hear whether Delta Metal (Lord Cadecote) will agree to send his donation through WRRC on our behalf, it has to be paid by charity credit. The group's new treasurer is Sasha Stenhoff (Hutchinson for professional purposes) she is a friend of Krissie Stephens' and was at Moor Court. I am the group secretary and co-signatory. (Holborough to McCormick, 1979c)

As DiCenzo identifies, for companies involved in the alternative theatre movement, 'It was common [...] to maintain some division of labour – making use of the skills and talents of individual members – but with a strong emphasis on preserving a democratic work environment' (1996: 56). Working as a co-operative still facilitated company members to lead in certain areas. As Holborough states, 'I mean it is true that Jenny and I did most of the admin, because I think we just wanted to keep powering it on, we didn't want it to stop' (Hicks and Holborough, 2020). The affirmation of Hicks and Holborough as founders in Clean Break's company narrative is, we argue, inextricably bound up with this *continuing* commitment to 'power it on', through undertaking the administrative work that supported the company to continue its artistic practice. For example, as the material held in the company's archive evidences, in the first decade of the organisation's existence the letters to trusts, funders and theatres are all from Hicks and Holborough, advocating for the work on behalf of the women.[5]

---

[5] Hicks also took up a part-time paid position with Women in Prison and with Creative and Supportive Trust (CAST), both ex-prisoner-led organisations, which allowed for collaboration of information and campaigning across all three organisations.

Beyond the artistic vision of the company, it is this volume of administrative labour that further affirms the pair as founders in the company narrative, the persistent grinding work of applying for funds, contacting venues and arranging accommodation. It is this labour that is captured in company records and thus becomes a legible part of its history.

The following selection of extracts from letters from Holborough to McCormick over the course of four months in 1980 illustrates something of the intermittent momentum of the early days of the company, indicative of the self-organising collective:

> Without new material and stronger (here comes that word again) commitment, I fail to see how we can make the Edinburgh Fringe again this year, or anywhere else other than the odd one-off date' (Holborough, 1980a).
> '[...] the group has split rather, with Jennifer rebuilding on the old ideals, two or three others thinking along variety-routines and me planning a one person play. All very amicable – this new direction is leading to a proposed sharing of the theatre space at this year's Edinburgh Festival under the general heading of Clean-Break but with three different projects (Holborough, 1980b).
>
> On a more confident note, we are musing over the National Tour following the festival. And then perhaps the American campus circuit. So if we can still dream it can't all be too bad. The administration is good too. Rowntree is giving us £200 this year [...] Another Trust, Hilden, wrote to me this week informing me that their Trustees were/are prepared to offer us £600. (Holborough, 1980c)

This commitment to keep powering the collective illuminates that founding is not just a single act, or an artistic vision, but a sustained and sustaining practice which, as Holborough's letters illustrate, can be challenging to bear because of material, political and personal circumstances. In histories and lineages of applied theatre it is important to recognise this more complex conceptualisation of founding, one that (in this instance) recognises the radical collective models of practice that are a significant antecedent to applied practice, while also acknowledging a temporally expanded understanding of founding as a practice that takes years. In this expanded iteration, founders inscribe themselves in company narratives not only through their artistic vision, but also through the administrative and material labour of driving a company forward. This is illuminated by the company's archive, the early years of which consist mainly of letters, budgets, funding applications, and newspaper clippings from Hicks and Holborough. As contemporary applied and community performance practices increasingly explore models of collective creation and a return to practices of cultural democracy is increasingly emphasised, it is useful to reiterate the significance of collectivity in the field's lineage and identify the ways in which such structures might affirm a particular politics, while also underscoring the need for members of any collective to take on roles to ensure the organisation is sustained.

Founding is not just the declaration of an idea – it is an iterative, enduring commitment to the realisation of it. The founding of Clean Break might then be understood as occurring over the course of a decade with Hicks and Holborough a constant energy behind the company during this period. Holborough left in 1986 to take up a writer-in-residence role at The Bush Theatre; Hicks, after cultivating funding and structures to secure a permanent home for the company, departed in 1990 to become the co-director of Women in Special Hospitals. As Hicks explained:

> I wanted to make sure that something was solid enough to have a future [...]. I stayed on another three or four years in terms of getting the long-term funding, achieving our first building and 15-year lease, [...]. I suppose all pioneers want a homestead somewhere. And there was a longer term involved, it wasn't any more short-term thinking because if we're going to pay wages and have people employed, things would [need to] change during that time. (Hicks and Holborough, 2020).

In this instance, founding then becomes a material act which Hicks articulates as creating a physical home for the company which has been a significant factor in Clean Break's endurance.

Figure 3 Clean Break Theatre Company with the Mayor of Camden outside HMP Holloway, 1986.

While there was a stable core of Clean Break Members throughout this founding decade – whose names are recorded in the archive but not the public histories of the company – there was also fluidity to the group. In the archival materials, there are around ten other women who emerge as key to the creative development of the company's work in their first decade: Eva Mottley, Sasha Hutchinson, Krissie Stephens, Caroline Needs, Susie Davies, Gwen, Cheryl, Sarah Newton, Adrienne McCloud, Lizzie Bristow, Jock Johnson and Chris Tchaikovsky. More broadly, Holborough stated in an interview with Susan Croft that the company worked with around fifty women during their first eight years (Croft, 2013). Some of the early company members left, having developed personal interests and professional skills (theatre and television writing, acting, teaching, therapy), others returned to prison, and some died, the result of drugs or suicide. By the late 1980s, the necessarily 'messy-collective' had dispersed and Clean Break became a theatre company with a management structure with discreet and designated roles. Increasingly Clean Break employed women who were sympathetic to the mission of the company rather than women who had personal experience of incarceration.

1.4 Company Narratives and National Agendas

Complicating the origin narrative of Clean Break expands understandings of what it might mean to found a theatre company and enables the company's position within the lineage of UK alternative theatre movement to become more explicit. Clean Break's body of work tracks against the wider priorities and parameters created by changes in cultural policies and funding, ideology and reception. In the late 1980s, Clean Break Women Prisoners Theatre Company became Clean Break Theatre Company. By dropping 'Women Prisoners' the company was explicitly acknowledging a change in the organisation's structures and decision-making practices. The collective of women with experience of prison became a company with employees whose politics aligned with the mission of the company, rather than women who had personal experience of criminalisation and incarceration. These fundamental changes were largely due to shifts in arts funding and wider theatre industry practices where hierarchical management models were normalised and expected.

In 1992 the company implemented a more structured staffing model following Alexandra Ford's appointment as Company Administrator. At the same time, the company also began to expand its education programme, starting with the writers in residence programme in 1993 and growing to include education and outreach strands from the early 2000s (see Section 2). Indeed, under the leadership of Lucy Perman (1997–2018), Clean Break's practice became synonymous with these education and outreach practices. During this period, the company hugely expanded its training provision for women in the community and its outreach work across different prison sites, as well as growing the artistic strand of its work. Positioning the work of the company as creating opportunities for artistic *and* personal development aligned with key funding principles in the UK arts sector in the early 2000s.

In this new model, strands of work were separated into 'Artistic' and 'Educational'. Clean Break commissioned plays from professional writers which were performed by professional actors, rather than being devised, written, and performed by women with lived experience of the criminal justice system or at risk of entering it. The Education programme primarily supported the personal and professional development of women, at this time termed Students (considered in Section 2). In the early 2010s, the sharp distinction between 'Artistic' and 'Education' was bridged through an 'Engagement' programme which involved centred on work with women who were incarcerated but also included writers in residence producing short plays, which were performed by Students.

In 2017, the commitment to collapse the boundaries between artistic, education, engagement and leadership strands of Clean Break's work, began the work of envisaging the most recent iteration of the company. Subsequently, in 2018 Clean Break underwent a significant restructure and refocused their work with women – now termed Members – to centre on their theatre practice. It is important to note that this was in part due to significant funding cuts at a local authority level, which contributed to the decision to close much of the education programme. Equally, in the cultural sector at this time there was an increasing turn to cultural democracy and collective theatre making. In this context of reduced funding and a turn to genuinely collaborative models of practice, Clean Break made a clear commitment to, once again, place Members' artistic work at the centre of the work the company do. Significantly for our discussion here, this change has shifted the articulation of the founders once again:

> Clean Break was set up in 1979 by two women who left prison determined to use theatre to tell their own stories and those of the women they met there. The new leadership team, inspired by the company's founding principles, will build a diverse community of women artists with lived experience of the criminal justice system [...] and leading and emerging theatre practitioners. (Perman, 2019)

It is notable that it is in this moment that the founders and their work are located within radical creative activism, which has once again become more legible in the company's articulation of its own past. While the focus on 'two women' remains, there is a recognition of other women and a desire to build a 'community of women artists'. This feels like an echo of the ambiguously collective beginnings of the company over forty years ago.

In sum, Clean Break's founding, and founding narrative, are important in several ways. Momentum was created and sustained by a group of people committed to a way of doing things for shared purposes. This was then sustained through the actions of two central individuals. Their responsibilities were essential to the establishment of Clean Break, but the way in which they were undertaken was subordinated to the idea of the collective and its aims. Scholars of applied and socially engaged theatre need to be aware of the prisms that origin stories are refracted through and attend to what they reveal about histories of work in this field. In Clean Break's case, this includes the articulation of the company as 'started by two women prisoners' offering the company legitimacy and authenticity during a period where social inclusion through cultural practice was being uncritically embraced. This disjuncture between the company's emergence as a collective and the centrality of Hicks and Holborough as co-founders in Clean Break's historicisation and contemporary articulations of the organisation's identity, provokes a wider consideration of the radical lineages of contemporary practices gathered under the umbrella term 'applied performance'.

2 Education as a Practice of Endurance

As we have established, Clean Break was created to directly address the patriarchal injustices of the criminal justice system. We have also shown that while theatre practices underpin all of Clean Break's work, specific approaches deployed by the company vary depending on the context of a particular historical moment. In this section, we focus on understanding the centrality of education to the company's longevity. The section begins with a brief overview of the structural changes to the company, as a framework for our primary focus on the concept of endurance as a way to understand Clean Break's education projects.

2.1 Structural Shifts, Education and Endurance

It was in the late 1980s that the company underwent a significant structural and ideological shift in how it operated. Draconian cuts to arts funding saw many theatre companies having to streamline operations; hierarchical management structures were normalised. In the case of Clean Break, this climate of economic hardship led to the dissolution of the collective as a working model (for both the creation and producing of work), which was replaced by an organisation of individuals with distinct and separate roles. This shift from a collective of prison-experienced theatre makers and activists to a professional theatre company with discrete areas of activity was particularly explicit in the separating out of the 'artistic' and 'educational' strands of the company's work.

Formerly, in the 1980s, the company ran education and training workshops for its Members. These included *Naming Ourselves,* a series of workshops led by Bonnie Greer 'specifically for women from ethnic minorities [. . .] to explore Black experience in a racist criminal justice system, as well as reclaiming past experience and the self'(Clean Break, 1989); *Stepping Out,* run in collaboration with Spare Tyre theatre company, attended to issues of life after release; and a *New Writing* programme, where a panel of theatre professionals, including Caryl Churchill and Timberlake Wertenbaker, offered critical feedback on work submitted by women with experience of prison (ibid). However, as the artistic programme developed with the commissioning of plays by professional writers, performed by actors, touring to regional theatres, the education programme focused specifically on developing programmes and structures of support in Clean Break's purpose-built, women-only centre in North London.

From the early 1990s until 2017, Clean Break developed a unique and (from the early 2000s) formally accredited education programme for women with experience of the criminal justice system. The company issued a range of diploma-equivalent qualifications, most consistently accredited by The Open College Network. At its height, the education programme consisted of over thirty courses. Some of these were more craft-focused – performance training such as Voice Skills, Movement for the Performer, Exploring Text, Audition Techniques (Access to Theatre 2008–9). Others focused on personal development and well-being – Self Development, Women and Anger, Making Choices, Improving your Mental Health (Clean Break, 2011). All of this was underpinned by responsive support staff who attended to the needs of Students and signposted other services beyond the expertise and capacity of the company. Women often came to the programme through a referral with a partner organisation (including women's centres, probation, hostels), prior contact with the company during a period of incarceration, or word of mouth.

In 2017, primarily due to swathes of funding cuts in local authority arts provision, national and European funding of arts and culture, alongside an increasing organisational focus on the role of Members within the organisation, Clean Break restructured their education and training provision in collaboration with the women who engaged with it. What emerged was a smaller and more theatre-making focused Members' Programme, committed to collapsing the boundaries between the artistic, education and engagement strands of Clean Break's work, which has shaped the most recent iteration of the company, with Members 'at the heart' of Clean Break. While the education, engagement, and now Members' Programme have been intrinsic to Clean Break's work since the early 1990s, a sustained exploration of this provision as a whole has not been undertaken in scholarship about the organisation. Instead, academic work has focused on individual courses within the programme (Bartley, 2019, 2022; Busby and Abraham, 2015; Merrill and Frigon, 2015; Walsh, 2019). In this section, we review Clean Break's education and engagement activities as a whole, identifying the personal and political work they do. This strand of Clean Break's work has been vital for the company's endurance, both in its political practice and viability as an organisation in the funding landscape of the early noughties. Specifically, we explore how education functions as a practice of endurance across the company's work.

In engaging with endurance as a central way to understand Clean Break's education programme, we reject the pervasive neoliberal language of developing individual resilience that has been utilised in policy and government agendas in relation to education and employment since the early 1990s. Endurance, as Julian Reid notes, has a spiritual and historical association with the capacity 'to bear pain and suffering, as well as have hope'; it is this tension between bearing pain and holding hope that we seek to engage with (Reid, 2022: 10). However, Reid also asserts that contemporary conceptualisations of endurance address the ways in which education systems 'train students in the endurance of otherwise intolerable conditions of life', and that this mode of education must be rejected in order to explore how 'the conditions of existence can be transformed rather than simply endured' (Reid, 2022: 11). In contrast, through engaging with Clean Break's work, we advocate for understanding the need for education projects that seek to engender transformation to practice and promote endurance as central to resistance.

Our analysis is informed by anthropologist Elizabeth A. Povinelli's (2011) work on endurance under the socially fragmented conditions of late liberalism. This mode of governance foregrounds a recognition of difference and alternative social worlds in order to deflect the critique of anti-neoliberal and anticolonial resistance. Povinelli's focus is predominantly on indigenous politics and socialites, but we draw on her work to interrogate systems of difference and disenfranchisement bound up in the criminalisation of women. We consider how Clean Break's education programme endures and trains endurance in order to create a space where women can imagine what Povinelli terms 'a social otherwise', an alternative to the existing structure of power and resources. A critical focus on endurance in this context seeks to illuminate the perseverance of trying to maintain the survival of alternative social realities at Clean Break under social conditions that seek to aggregate social worlds and manage resistance.

2.2 Five Decades of Arts and Criminal Justice

As the longest running theatre and criminal justice organisation in the UK, Clean Break have endured an increasingly hostile arts funding landscape and successive waves of punitive justice policies. Here, we reflect on how they have persisted through continuous action. Povinelli utilises the term 'tense' to refer to how an event's temporality is narrated to signify or enact control. In the carceral society that Clean Break intervenes in we understand this tense in relation to both 'doing time' while incarcerated and also the ways in which criminalisation has an extended temporality, one which operates beyond a prison sentence and serves to marginalise people with lived experience of incarceration. We are particularly interested in the longevity of the organisation and how this has supported women involved in the education programme to endure the structural violence of the criminal legal system. As Povinelli asserts, 'Internal to the concept of endurance (and exhaustion) is the problem of substance: its strength, hardiness, callousness; its continuity through space; its ability to suffer and yet persist' (2011: 32). We can point to Clean Break's hardiness – there have been difficult decisions – and recognise that its continuance over five decades has been a site of struggle, rather than an inevitability in the field of arts and criminal justice. As previous company member and long-time collaborator Paulette Randall identifies:

> The thing is, when you think back to the late seventies, early eighties there were so many other fringe theatre companies in London at that time. There was the women's committee at the GLC, you were supported by Ken Livingstone and [...] people who supported the arts, and it meant that you were kind of fearless and felt that of course you could do whatever you wanted to do because you were being supported. [...] [W]hen that started to change then, of course, other things have to play a bigger part in what you're trying to do. A lot of companies went by the wayside, Clean Break is still here, so ... You know, testimony to them to being able to change in the way that you have to in order to survive. (Randall, 2020)

That Clean Break has continued to exist, while so many of their peer organisations have not, which is remarkable. Randall's comments are echoed by Clean Break Member Artist Sylvia Amanquah, 'Honestly, because there is a lot of companies that are no longer here. And I know that Clean Break has gone through a lot. There is times where they've really had to kind of fight to keep going' (2020). In taking up endurance we foreground the work of this continuance. When companies have been around for decades this organisational persistence is, we argue, overlooked or taken for granted; such companies begin to feel like an implicit part of the sector. As Randall and Amanquah both assert,

Clean Break changed in order to survive in the shifting landscape of arts practice from the early 1990s. The ability of the company to respond to the changing political, economic and cultural landscape can be traced through the shifts and changes in their education programme and in the material site it operates within.

A central feature of the company's endurance is its building, a material space in which its education programmes could grow and flourish. As long-term Clean Break collaborator Vishni Velada Billson notes, the education programme

> wasn't about a [...] rehabilitative concept, it was about this beautiful light building, with food, with support, with housing help, with women – other women who are really prepared to put their [...] creativity and emotional support behind you. And so, the whole programme really was this [...] guiding structured light that was there to support any woman who'd been through the criminal justice system [...] who could arrive here and be held for a while. (Velada Billson, 2020)

As previously noted, Jenny Hicks was intent on getting the company into a building in order to give it a home (see Section 1.3). In its early

Figure 4 Clean Break Building at Night, photographer unknown

days, Clean Break's work – the planning, fundraising, meetings, workshops, rehearsals and eating together – all took place in the cramped but vibrant offices across the borough of Camden that Hicks had first located. In the late 1980s and early 1990s fundraising began for a dedicated, women-only space. In 1995, with the support of Lottery and Arts Council funding, a derelict building – once a piano factory and a tie factory – off Kentish Town high street was bought. Clean Break's brief to the architects, Avanti, articulates the vision for the building:

> The organisation was founded and first organised on self-help principles and continues to involve Students at all levels. Therefore, it is essential that the building does not feel intimidating or appear institutional. Clean Break's clients are often vulnerable, sometimes volatile and frequently damaged by institutionalisation. The building should respond and acknowledge this – it should be bright, soft, open and honest. (Avanti, 1995)

The building is bright and open. It has high ceilings, walls of glass, lots of windows and you can see and hear bodies as they circulate through it, as they pause to have conversations, as they travel up the stairs, across the corridors, in the 'green room' and each of the three studios. A kitchen, offices and smaller meeting rooms connect the spaces between the studios. Outside, a garden courtyard. The space – outside and in – is, to quote Avanti, 'light and set out in an ordered and legible fashion .... Mak[ing] architectural use of those notions which are at the core of the company's educational philosophy – discovery, security, illumination and transformation' (ibid).

This articulation of values that underpinned the design of the building set the tone for an approach to being together, to working together, which is not only the antithesis of carceral spaces but a commitment to alternative ways of being and working. This stands in direct contrast to the prison estate as the material fabrication of ideology – 'a product of power relations, cultural and social dynamics, [...] everyday values and meanings' (Hayward, 2012, 441). Clean Break – the building – is also the material fabrication of ideology where 'everyday values and meanings' continue to be meticulously, carefully, collaboratively reflected on and shaped by the company. Crew et al. (2013) drawing on human and carceral geography consider space and place as 'determinants of social practice and personal experience, rather than an empty theatre or neutral backcloths within and against which they occur' (60). Interviews with over seventy Members, staff, associate artists, and Board Members (past and present), are exuberant in detailing how their experiences of the building are shaped not only by the architecture, but also by the social practices and relationships created over time within it. As Member artist Peaches Cadogan notes:

> the buildings still have that same soul, like I've never even left, you know. For me that's priceless. I still feel like [...] if I was going through struggles, I could still come to this building and say look, this is what's going on, you know. And I'm just blessed to know that we have a place like this [...] I don't want people to think that, yeah, prison changed her. No, it wasn't prison, it was having an establishment and being linked to somewhere that actually understood me and supported me on my journey going forward. It wasn't prison, it was having a place like Clean Break. Clean Break by name, Clean Break by nature, no judgement. (Cadogan, 2020)

In the building, the company has created an alternative space to support endurance. As previous CEO Lucy Perman noted in 2019:

> it's been a really difficult couple of decades, and yet you wouldn't know that if you came into the Clean Break building or worked with the women there. It's probably the most joyful, hopeful, optimistic environment I've ever worked in, because of the women themselves, and there's a lot that we can now learn and a lot the government can learn from actually talking directly to women who've been through the system and asking them what they need and how they can be supported to get their lives back on track. Because they have the most extraordinary resilience, most extraordinary fighting spirit, and they often know what they need. (Perman, 2019)

The UK government's decision to pursue a politics of austerity from 2010 was keenly felt within the criminal justice system and by organisations occupying the arts landscape. Clean Break and the women it works with have endured acutely different economic, social and cultural landscapes. As Labour MP David Lammy asserted, the part-privatisation of the probation service during this period 'was the deepest privatisation that the criminal justice system has ever experienced, it transferred 70% of the work done by the public probation service to private and voluntary sector providers' (UK Parliament, 2020). Given the scarcity of support from under-resourced private probation services, Clean Break's education programme became an even more necessary resource. As Perman's quote recognises, in this context, to have a building and programme that makes space for women to fight for an alternative, is vital.

2.3 Training Theatre Makers

We argue that Clean Break's education practices have been fundamental to its survival; both economically (in terms of enabling the company to access to shifting funding streams) and ideologically (in relation to sustaining its commitment to centring women with lived experience of the criminal justice system). The foregrounding of Clean Break's educational and engagement work during the 1990s and early 2000s, enabled the company to make its mission legible to local government and cultural funders during this period. Throughout the 1980s, Clean Break had undertaken advocacy work and collectively worked on creating and touring productions. The increasing shift to professionalisation at Clean Break in the early 1990s, in the running of the company and the creatives they employed, was a significant driver in the emergence of the training company. As minutes for a 1992 management committee meeting note:

> there had been a change in the company's work, which means that it aims more at enabling ex-prisoners as opposed to employing ex-prisoners at all levels. It was felt that this change has been very appropriate and had to happen. (Clean Break, 14 May 1992)

The creation of the training programme, therefore, provided a space for women to develop their artistic practice and enabled the company to fulfil its central commitment to fostering creative opportunities for women with experience of the criminal justice system.

In 1991 and 1992 Clean Break ran ten-week pilots of a performance training programme, funded by the London Arts Board. This was a three-day-a-week programme, supporting Students to develop performance skills and culminating in a collaboratively devised production performed at the Clean Break premises which included *The Survivor* (1991), and *Sexing Venus* (1992). Students were given travel and subsistence expenses, as well as access to a crèche during class. One of the early ambitions of this programme was for the company to be 'able to train its own cast members' (Clean Break, 1992a: 17). During the early 1990s it became regular company practice to blend Members and professionals, which in some ways is echoed by the model that Clean Break is returning to in the 2020s. Sarah Daniels' *Head-rot Holiday* (1992) included one woman who had experience of a secure psychiatric unit, and one who had been on the company's training programme. The production's programme noted: 'Particularly talented participants can join the professional company, becoming a member of the cast or an assistant in the production team. From this they can receive up to three months' work and an Equity card' (Clean Break, 1992). A total of five women with lived experience of the justice system received Equity cards from the company during 1991/92. Two women from the training programme became Assistant Stage Managers and one was Assistant Director. Four went on to further work in the theatre, and one started training to work with young people in theatre. The programme itself included poetry written by women who had been or were still held in special hospitals and secure psychiatric units and was illustrated by

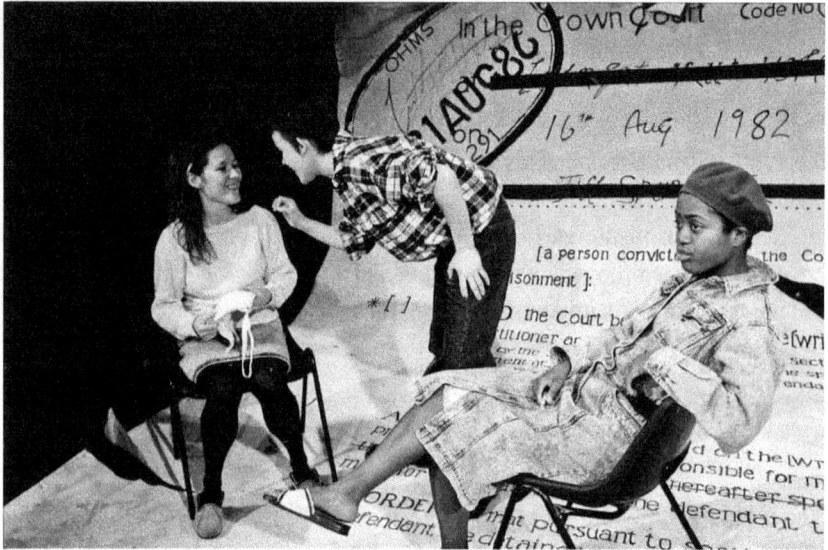

Figure 5 1992 – *Head-Rot Holiday* (1992) by Sarah Daniels. Photograph by Sarah Ainslie

a woman who had been held in Holloway's C1 psychiatric wing, whose painting was chosen for the publicity for *Head-Rot Holiday*. Indeed, some of the women embraced the training programme in particular as an opportunity for artistic development, with one student feeding back 'Since then I have worked on two short films and a play and earned my Equity card' and another going on to feature in the company's 1994 production *Red* (Training Programme Review, 1995). Others spoke of the course as an opportunity to develop their ability to 'work in a group and have more patience' (ibid). These dual outcomes of the very first training programme, artistic upskilling and personal development, would underpin much of the provision on offer at Clean Break for the next twenty-five years.

Following this pilot, in 1993 the Home Office provided the company with a funding increase from £15,000 to £42,000. This led to an expansion of the Training Programme to include an Introductory Performance Arts course, a ten-week Training Company Performance Course, and a year-long Further Acting Course (accredited through London Open College Federation). The titles of these courses changed over time and a clear progression route through the programme was developed.[6] The introduction and expansion

---

[6] There were also progression opportunities with several students taking up placements with the organisation and contributing to the day-to-day running of the company. This programme

of these performance courses formed the basis of what became the onsite Education Programme; specifically, the Training Company was the antecedent for two strands of work that became core to Clean Break's provision: the Access to Higher Education Course (Access) and the Graduate Touring Work.

Between 1993 and 2011, The Access Course offered a Level 3 Qualification – equivalent to 2 A Levels[7] – accredited by Open College Network. There were twelve places on the course annually and it ran three days a week in line with the academic year. City and Islington College sub-contracted Clean Break to deliver Access as a 'progression route from its entry level accredited courses'.[8] As former Head of Engagement, Imogen Ashby noted:

> the significance actually of the Access course was how really transformative it was for everyone. I think that's one of the things that struck me, it wasn't just transformative for the women, it was really transformative for staff as well. And that's partly because of the support structures that were in place. I mean we had a lot of supervision. There was a real recognition that in order to deliver this kind of interesting work, staff had to be well supported. People really changed, you know, you really witnessed people really transform their lives. (ibid.)

In creating a supportive space for women to explore their theatre-making practice and ensuring staff were fully supported in facilitating this process, the company was able to foster a diversification of voices accessing higher education and the theatre sector, cultivating different perspectives on the criminalisation of women.

The work produced by and with Access Students experimented with genre, diverging from the stark realism that characterised much of Clean Break's Student work. To exemplify: Zawe Ashton's fantastical *She from the Sea* (2010) performed by Students on the Access Course follows three women – Pearl, Masha and Edlin – who live together by the sea. The trio remember nothing of their lives before and make the best of their collective solitude and calm retreat, eating what they dredge out of the water – tin cans, newspaper, fish

---

developed, finally linking up with the sector-wide Stage Works scheme, which thirty-eight women participated in taking up ninety-three placements in total.

[7] Short for Advanced Levels, A Levels are qualifications within the UK national curriculum for students post-16 education. They are not compulsory. They can lead to further training, work or university.

[8] There was also a strong relationship with the Royal Central School of Speech and Drama through their widening participation agenda, which guaranteed Clean Break students interviews for the undergraduate Drama, Applied Theatre and Education programme.

heads. Then Marina washes up in their fishing nets and is pulled ashore, raving about being held below the water for years:

> MARINA: There are giant oysters down there that suck you in
> and keep you in their
> mouths for days, months, years!
> Years without light! Only bits of pearl to eat!
>
> (Ashton, 2010: 11)

Pearl, Masha and Edlin take this mysterious woman in and she helps them to fish and feed one another, she sings and gradually the others find their voices. This harmony is abruptly shattered when a fisherwoman bursts into their commune seeking revenge on Marina, who claims she killed her child. It emerges that Marina has been in the ocean for five years, punishment for her alleged crime:

> MARINA: I have been to the bottom of the ocean.
> I have learned to hold my breath for over two days.
> I swam for so long that parts of my breasts grew scales and the ribs on
>   my right side
> sometimes cracked apart to become gills.
> I dodged sharks and hungry whales.
> And I have made it to the shore.

Figure 6 *She from the Sea* (2010) by Zawe Ashton, Photographer Tracey Anderson

Somehow I have made it to the shore again.
Even with my hands tied.
I didn't drown.
I didn't drown.
I didn't drown.
I didn't drown.
I didn't drown.

(ibid: 27–28)

Ashton's use of the sea and the shore in *She from the Sea* invokes the exhaustion of incarceration, the fight to survive against all the odds, and the potential of a group of women collectively sustaining one another offers a powerful analogy. Being at sea, drowning, tied hands, and making it to the shore all offer a creative language that communicates the effect of being entangled in the justice system and the potential of collective gathering to find an alternative future.

The Access Students performed a range of productions at different sites in London: *Five Go to Hollywood* (devised by Clean Break Students, 2005) was performed in HMP Holloway; *Cakehole* (Lucy Kirkwood, 2008), an exploration of the social and legal oppression of lesbian and trans identities and the impact of such violence on characters' lives, was produced at The Hampstead Theatre; and the final production prior to the closure of the Access Course was *Cleaning Up* (Winsome Pinnock, 2011) staged at the Oval House Theatre and followed three women working as cleaners in an office at the heart of London's financial district.

During this period, the company also ran First Stage (2006–7), a shorter-lived but similar intervention in the theatre landscape, which was a practical traineeship for Black and Asian women in stage management, sound and lighting and all technical areas of theatre. The course was for anyone working in the industry and had one ring fenced place for a Clean Break student. It ran as a two-week intensive at Clean Break's base, followed by a traineeship (a supported placement) at London venues, including The Royal Court, The Young Vic and National Youth Theatre, Theatre Royal Stratford East, and the Tricycle. The traineeships were paid and supported by a personal mentor; the aim was for trainees to gain the necessary skills to secure employment in their area of specialism. Such programmes make interventions that are often imperceptible at a macro scale, but through the endurance of the provision offered by Clean Break the women involved were able to access systems and structures previously inaccessible to them. Until 2017, the company also ran courses in partnership with other higher education providers (London College of Fashion, make-up for theatre course; Rose Bruford College, backstage course;

Royal Central School of Speech and Drama, Discover Higher Education course and The Summer School). This partnership working also makes a tangible intervention in who those organisations are addressing and how they are developing their own pedagogies.

The other heir to Clean Break's first Training Programme was the Graduate Touring Work. In 1995, then Education Co-Ordinator, Pauline Gladstone, proposed the introduction of a tour of the students' work that emerged from the now extensive performance programmes. This proposal was widely supported in the organisation, particularly because it further addressed the lack of representation of women with lived experience in mainstage shows as the company moved through the 1990s. It was thought that this: 'would resolve problems with professional cast not being ex-offenders and could be achieved with 1/5 of the professional budget reallocated to it. [...] The members of that second level Training Company would be in an ideal position to audition for the professional company' (Clean Break Management Committee minutes, 1 June 1995).

As the minutes evidence, the introduction of the Training Company creating and touring work as part of the yearly programme was initially proposed as an economically efficient way to create opportunities for women with lived experience to develop their theatre-making practice. In this format, the Training Company was envisaged as a way to sustain the flow of women who had been through the criminal legal system into mainstage productions – supporting them to develop their skills and then audition for the 'Professional Company' shows.

When Lucy Morrison joined the company as Head of Artistic Programming in 2005, she further embedded the playwrights Clean Break worked with as part of this touring work:

> I wanted the writers here to be as resident as possible and it was just an absolute no-brainer for me that they would write for the Students to perform, [...] I do think there's nothing quite like having a purpose, a text written for a specific group of performers that you know what their skills are and perhaps what their weaknesses are, and you know how to make them shine. [...] just wanting those Students to have that feeling of having the right line written for them or the character that they just get. (Morrison, 2020)

What became known as The Graduate Tour, ran in this format annually from 2008 until 2016, involving graduates of the company's performance course collaborating with a writer on a short production. Students who had been through the performance programmes would audition to be involved in the production, which would normally consist of a small cast of between three and six women. What became distinctive about Clean Break's graduate work was the way in which these productions directly sought to stimulate dialogue around the experiences of women caught up in the criminal legal system. The productions were always accompanied by a workshop, which offered space for audiences to work through the material and engage with the complexities of the experiences depicted. Much of this work toured to prisons, universities, government agencies, third sector and charity organisations working in justice, health, education and women's spaces.

While there were tight parameters around the length and scale of the work, there was significant diversity and depth in the themes and forms that these plays experimented with. Some indicative examples include: *Missing Out* (Mary Cooper, 2008), depicts the experiences of the families of imprisoned women; *Sweatbox* (Chloe Moss, 2015), encloses audiences in a claustrophobic prison van as three women are transported from court to prison; *Spent* (Katherine Chandler, 2016), stages three women's struggle to survive under the UK government's austerity agenda; and Sonya Hayle's *Hours 'til Midnight* (2012), explores addiction from the perspective of two sisters and was the first graduate commission written by a Member Artist. Across these works, playwrights draw on different formal strategies to interrogate the realities of criminalisation that they address. For example, Vivienne Franzmann's *Sounds Like an Insult* (2015), uses a series of short snapshots, some direct address, and other vignettes of dialogue to explore the experiences of women with complex mental health needs within the criminal legal system:

> Scene 1: Samantha (B)
> B looks at a report in her hands. A&C are prison officers.
> B: (to audience) I said to him, I said, yeah, but what is it? And he said
> A: I don't know.
> B: (to A) What does it mean?
> A: I was just told to give you the report.
> C: He was just told to give you the report.
> B: Yeah, but, it says here
> C: We've got to go
> B: I don't know what this is.
> A: I can't help you. I was just
> B: But, it says here that I
> C: We've got to go to the other wing.
> B: It says .... (gives A the report) Here. That's what they're saying about me.

A: I don't know anything about it.
B: (points at the paper) That.
C: We've got to go.
A: I don't know
B: It says
C: You should ask someone in mental health.
B: It says-
A: I was just told to give you the report.
B: Personality Disorder.
A: I was just told to
B: Sounds like an insult.
C: He was just told to give you the report.
B: Sounds like a bloody insult.

(Franzmann, 2015: 1–2)

This is the first scene of the play and is representative of the brief insight audiences are given into a character's experience before attention shifts to a different situation in a new scene. These brief encounters include scenes of staccato dialogue (as already mentioned), alongside short monologues voicing different characters' experiences. As Franzmann reflected:

> the form of that play is 13 short scenes in 20 minutes and they're all different characters, and that felt like the form came from all the research, there's no one response to that diagnosis. Everyone has a different response, some people are relieved to get that diagnosis, some people are horrified. (Ashby and Franzmann, 2020)

The collage form of the play reflected the diversity of experience in the system and, further, in its fast-moving and constantly changing style created the effect of being in a constantly moving landscape that was difficult to gain a foothold in – a failing system in disarray.

Both *Sounds Like an Insult* and *She from the Sea* depict women enduring the system and are indicative of ways in which Clean Break's Student productions sought to create performances that would enable audiences accessible ways into complex conversations about incarceration and criminalisation. This work was the beginning of intentional and structural blurring of the boundaries between education and professional strands of practice with the students performing this work in a range of professional contexts, both in theatres and festivals (LIFT, Oval House, Soho Theatre and Latitude Festival) and criminal justice, health and third-sector organisations.

2.4 Everydayness and the Work of the Education Programme

Prior to the merging of the artistic and educational strands of Clean Break's work in 2017, there was a persistent tension and a perceived hierarchy of resource and attention embedded in the artistic work (AKA the 'professional' productions that were often co-produced with major UK theatres) and the education, outreach and graduate practice of the organisation. Here we turn to Povinelli's conceptualisation of 'eventfulness', which connotes an interest in both amplified encounters with crisis or catastrophe but also, and more commonly, those events that are not deemed significant enough to be termed eventful. It is these 'quasi-events' that Povinelli is keen to attend to, the 'ordinary, chronic, and cruddy rather than catastrophic, crisis-laden, and sublime', in order to advocate that we reorient who is perceived as in need of support and how we respond (2011: 13). Here she is talking about the everydayness of marginalised people's increased exposure to harm. We deploy Povinelli's dichotomy of the event (as catastrophic rupture) and the quasi-event (as small breakages and struggles assigned as ordinary); casting the mainstage productions as dealing with the frame of 'the event' and the education work as navigating the quasi-events encountered by women in the criminal justice system. In drawing on the 'quasi-event', we argue that the education work at Clean Break over thirty years persistently and doggedly addressed the everyday and the chronic experiences of those encountering the carceral system. Unlike the plays, that implicitly centre a particular crisis event to be witnessed by an audience, the education work attended to the ongoing and unrecognised violence that women with lived experience encountered.

In this context of recognising the violence encountered by the women they work with, Clean Break centres trauma-informed practice in their work. The company draws on Stephanie Covington's work in this area, which encourages organisations to:

> take the trauma into account; avoid triggering trauma reactions or retraumatising the woman; adjust the behaviour of counsellors and custodial staff members to support the woman's coping capacity; allow survivors to manage their trauma symptoms successfully, so that they are able to access, retain, and benefit from the services. (Covington, 2014: 2)

Beyond ensuring staff are trained in trauma-informed practice, Clean Break accounts for the potential experiences of trauma within their Membership by fostering supportive spaces for the women to make work. Members attending Clean Break are cared for by the Members' Support Team who work with the women to support them through emotional, logistical or financial difficulties that might arise during their engagement with the company. This support might consist of counselling, advice around housing or employment, and signposting to wider services. Clean Break therefore embed their trauma-informed approach both within workshop practice and in the wider fabric of the organisation, as Ashby notes: 'all of our work was trauma informed, because it was all about recognising where somebody was meeting you in their relational engagement and seeing what you could do with that' (Ashby and Franzmann, 2020). In having a trauma-informed practice, Clean Break is making space to make present and legible the unperceived quasi-events that erode access to imagining other lives or accessing a position of agency.

In 2000, the Self Development Programme was created by Clean Break education staff member, Fay Barratt, and self-development facilitator Jackee Holder, for women not ready to move on to theatre courses provided by Clean Break but keen to engage with the company and access support around health, well-being, interpersonal skills and personal growth. The programme grew under the stewardship of Anna Herrmann (Head of Education, 2002–18) and Imogen Ashby (Education Manager 2002–10; and Head of Engagement 2011–16). This expansion of provision, moving beyond performance practice, asserted the role of Clean Break as a leading provider in London for women with convictions. A complementary strand to the company's Self Development Programme was the Women and Anger Course, which was a structured group-work programme written by a psychotherapist and comprised of fifteen sessions delivered over six weeks. It was created 'for women who find it difficult to express their anger in a way which is not harmful to themselves or to others', and women completed a pre-assessment with the Student Support team in order to gauge their suitability for the programme (Clean Break, 2015). Women and Anger was founded in Social Learning theory and employed Cognitive Behavioural methods to address the relatively under explored area of women's feelings of anger through facilitated group sessions (Clarke and Williams, 2005). The course aimed to provide 'a non-judgmental space for you to understand your anger, manage your emotions better and to practise new coping strategies through drama techniques and creative practice' (Clean Break, 2015). While the company had experience of creating well-being and personal development courses, Women and Anger was distinctive in that it was the company's first structured group-work programme to address emotional and behavioural factors. The programme was delivered to ten women in each cycle with facilitators guided by a manual, specialist training, and supervision. The Women and Anger course ran until the closure of the education programme creating a space for women to come together collectively and creatively to work through experiences of anger and develop coping strategies for triggering situations. As one participant fed back at the end of the course:

> someone from my past who I used to use drugs with, he continually called me asking to meet. I felt furious with him. I shared it in the group and we did an exercise where I had to take a different course of action. I went home that day and he called and I was able to tell him not to call me again. It was important for me to do that as I know the consequences if I had remained silent. (cited in Clarke and Williams, 2005)

Women and Anger is indicative of the suite of well-being and personal development programmes that Clean Break offered during this period, which sought to equip women with tools to navigate the various 'quasi-events' they might encounter and which might lead them into further contact with the criminal legal system.

These examples of Clean Break's direct development programmes are closely allied to their other engagement work, much of which is offered with women held in prison settings and is structured around the playwriting residencies that Clean Break have developed. Playwrights are resident with the company for around eighteen months, occasionally longer, during which time they do a series of projects at different prisons and also access creative support for writers by building relationships with commissioning theatres. Again, this process was formalised by Lucy Morrison when she joined the company. During this residency playwrights draw on their collaborations with Members and women they work with in prison to write a commission for the company, either a shorter touring piece (around thirty minutes) to be performed by Clean Break Members in different professional settings (probation services, prisons, universities) or the company might collaborate with a larger producing theatre towards a full-length production. Often resident playwrights do both. The majority of the work in prison settings then is focused on playwriting and performance sharings among the incarcerated women. The residencies predominantly occur in a three-day block, with Clean Break artists working with a group of women facilitating exercises on theatre writing and supporting them to create their own work. At the end of the project, actors come in and perform the women's work back to them or they can perform it alongside the actors if they want to. There is a focus on creating an opportunity for women to see their own work performed. As Anna Herrmann notes 'within those three days it's very possible to create a different culture within the prison for them, and that's a really powerful starting point' (Herrmann quoted in Drinkwater and Davey, 2017: 4). Through this small intervention then, there can be the beginnings of a shift in the experience of what can happen in a prison site. Reflecting on the impact of this work in prisons, Morrison noted:

> We'd only be here [at a prison] for a few days, but people would say it had sort of changed their lives. I mean it was kind of slightly spooky in a way, it's partly because prison is so kind of barren that you go in with quite a small offering and it becomes really transformative. [...] it's partly because, you know, people are starved in all senses of the word. (Morrison, 2020)

There was an 'everydayness' in the work that the company did in different prison settings, 'small offerings' in contained projects that made minor interventions in bringing performance into carceral spaces. However, in doing this work consistently and taking theatre into these 'barren' sites, the work enabled a kind of experience of endurance for those participating.

In her analysis of endurance as a practice of performance art, Lara Shalson notes that '[e]ndurance is thus a wilful act, but a wilful act that confronts in repeated and sustained encounters the limits of individual agency' (2018: 13). There is a wilfulness to Clean Break's education and engagement programmes, which support women to confront their encounters with, in this instance quite literally, their limited agency. While the work of the mainstage productions was significant in advocating for criminalised women, depicting crises that they might encounter and trying to expand wider understandings of these contexts, the ongoing and persistent work of the education programme at Clean Break supported women to navigate the imperceptible quasi-events that further marginalise and oppress them. In addressing the quasi-event through their education programme, Clean Break dealt with 'how the very nature of the quasi-event makes it an effective means for shifting accountability away from neoliberalism onto those who suffer in neoliberalism' (Povinelli, 2011: 154). In brief, the education and engagement work supported women to navigate and name the oppressive structures they encountered.

2.5 'The Women': From Company, to Students, to Members

When in conversation with anyone involved in the work of Clean Break they often refer to 'the women', to reference the women whom the organisation seeks to serve, stand alongside and advocate for through performance. An exploration of the education and outreach strand of Clean Break's work is significant as it offers an opportunity to reflect on the position of women with lived experience of the criminal justice system over the company's history and to consider what this means for the company's practice and wider understandings of socially and politically committed theatre making. In what has preceded, we have traced the shift of women with lived experience from founders to company members, to students, to graduates. Read alongside Povinelli's framing of endurance, which asks us to critique who is empowered to assert the structures through which we construct our morality and ethics, a consideration of how women with lived experience are positioned at Clean Break invites a reflection on who gets to shape how the organisation presents criminalised women.

In 2017, the education programme (as outlined earlier) ceased. What has emerged subsequently is a reimagining of the company and its relationship with women with lived experience of the criminal justice system. In the press release stating this shift in Clean Break's work, they announced a new mission: 'Producing ground-breaking theatre which puts women's voices at its heart and creates lasting change by challenging injustice in and beyond the criminal justice system' (Herrmann in Clean Break, 2018). This intention to centre women's voices was to be realised by a new model of practice, central to which was a Members' programme: 'In the new model, Members (previously students and graduates) will join the company, engage in high quality training and workshops and participate in Clean Break's creative life. The Members will be at the heart of our theatre output and vision for: A society where women can realise their full potential, free from criminalisation' (Herrmann in Clean Break, 2018).

In 2019, the company produced *Inside Bitch*, conceived by Stacey Gregg and Deborah Pearson, and devised and performed by Clean Break Members Lucy Edkins, Jennifer Joseph, TerriAnn Oudjar and Jade Small. It was a powerful first public manifestation of this reimagined mission. Co-produced with The Royal Court, *Inside Bitch* was the realisation of the mission to put Members centre stage, marking a notable development of the practice of the Graduate Touring work discussed earlier, with Edkins, Joseph, Oudjar and Small all contributing to the development of the performance, which reached mainstage audiences over its month-long run (see also Section 3). Subsequently, Clean Break has produced mixed-cast productions, with several Members appearing in *[Blank]* (at The Donmar Warehouse, 2019), *Typical Girls* (at The Crucible Theatre, 2021), and *Dixon and Daughters* (The National Theatre of Great Britain, 2023) working alongside actors without lived experience of the criminal justice system.

During the first year of the COVID-19 pandemic, Clean Break produced *2 Metres Apart*, a project that paired 12 artists with 12 Clean Break Member Artists to undertake eight weeks of creative collaboration. This signified the increasing commitment to co-creation at the company and the continuing erosion of boundaries that had previously existed between professional artists and women with lived experience within the company's work. The work *2 Metres Apart* itself was not focused on a commissioning process or geared towards producing work, but instead sought to offer opportunities for creative collaborations to emerge during a period of social isolation. Anna Herrmann has described the project as 'the clearest example of a project in which we were looking to further our investment in collaboration, which is in a way a follow up to *Inside Bitch*' (Herrmann qtd in Bartley, 2021: 84). The increasing diversification of the ways in which work is created, produced and shared with audiences by Clean Break has been rooted in the company's commitment to finding new models of co-operation and collaboration that reassert the value of different forms of knowledge and across different experiences. This echoes an increasing turn to the reassertion of the value of lived experience and the appeal of co-creation in the current arts landscape. This refocusing of Clean Break's work prioritises the knowledge of those who have been through the system, increasingly positioning the women as authors and performers of their own experience and, in Povinelli's framework, as central to narrativising the ways in which women are criminalised.

It is important to note that while this recentring of women with lived experience in the artistic work of the company is a shift in the way it organises its creative practice, the women have been central to the ethical work of the organisation throughout their history. An example of Clean Break's commitment to centring the voices and experiences of women with lived experience was *Breaking In* (1999–2001). This was a two-year training project that worked with Members to develop their skills as community-theatre facilitators. The programme specifically aimed to train Members to work with young people deemed 'at risk' of offending and more broadly with other marginalised communities, which had an increased likelihood of coming into contact with the criminal justice system. The project included onsite training at Clean Break and also traineeships working in different community organisations and prisons. There were eleven trainees who completed the course, with several completing portfolios for a Level 3 NVQ in Delivering Art Form Development Sessions. As is stated on Clean Break's digital archive website: '[t]he project was unique in its aspiration to ensure that theatre practice in criminal justice settings was led by those with experience of the system themselves' (Clean Break, 'Short Courses and Progression Routes', n.d.). This work, coinciding with a period of increased professionalisation in community arts practice, offered training to enable Members to be positioned as practitioners in arts and criminal justice projects rather than just participants. Such a move is significant in terms of disrupting who gets to design, create and lead work in arts and criminal justice contexts.

Clean Break is a company that persistently addresses and intervenes in systems of power in the work it produces. Members increasingly have a structural say in the decision-making process by which writers are commissioned and are more regularly appearing and/or contributing to the creation of the main stage work. However, there is a need for checking the optimism which such transformative modes of creation seem to offer. In 2022 Clean Break ran four courses: Health and Wellbeing, Creative Space, Theatre Makers, and Writers Room at their site in Kentish Town. Therefore, in practice Clean Break now run a significantly reduced provision for women, with fewer courses that focus predominantly on theatre-making provision for women with lived experience. The removal of funds for this work attests to the erosion of the culture sector. More broadly there is a continued lack of local authority funding for cultural provision following over a decade of austerity policies, the COVID-19 pandemic, the energy crisis, and inflationary pressures and insufficient economic support from the UK government leading to a cost-of-living crisis, which has put acute pressures on public services. Finally, the withdrawal of the UK from the European Union has had significant impacts on those organisations previously in receipt of EU funding.

Current Artistic Director, Anna Herrmann, reaffirms Clean Break's ongoing commitment to endurance: 'We must continue to be there for generations to come, to celebrate more successes and to make sure that the door continues to stay open' (Herrmann, 2013: 335). Indeed, as we have observed, one of the most significant things about Clean Break is its longevity over the course of forty plus years. The restructuring of the company as Member-focused is a manifestation of the ways in which the company transforms to persist; hopefully this will enable it to continue to deliver provision for women with lived experience for decades to come. As former CEO Lucy Perman said when reflecting on her own role as a leader at the company,

> I felt that my responsibility was to make it okay for the organisation to live with uncertainty, in the way that the women that we've worked with live constantly with uncertainty. You know, they may not know how they're going to feed their children the next day, they may not know what's going to be the outcome of a court case. Actually, the organisation does have some certainty. [...] it has a building, it has some funding, it has a wonderful staff team, a board of directors, and so on, and it makes wonderful work. But there's a lot of unknown and I think I grew in confidence at being able to say, I don't know what the future holds, but let's find out together and let's work collaboratively to make the organisation able to adapt and thrive and survive, no matter what happens around it. (Perman, 2019)

In this section, we have explored endurance through three frames: (1) the longevity of the company as temporal endurance; (2) the focus of the training company on sustaining opportunities for women with lived experience and the ways in which the wider education programme addressed everyday 'ordinary' violences; and (3) what shifts in the location of women with experience reveal about how the company contests who gets to formulate ethical and moral codes under the logic of late liberalism. By foregrounding endurance, we have sought to recognise the ways the company, and the women it works with, navigate the different uncertainties that surround cultural institutions and carceral contexts in ways that enable it to survive in an increasingly hostile landscape. This offers a way to understand how the persistence of the company as a whole, and its education programme in particular, intervenes in the ways in which the temporalities, systems of categorising an event's significance, and the moral structures of our society further disenfranchise marginalised communities. In sum, an organisation such as Clean Break tries to create social alternatives through which we can collaboratively imagine new moral realities.

3 Facts, Fictions and Narratives of Knowing in Carceral Society

On the stage of the Royal Court's Jerwood Theatre Upstairs, four women change into lime green jumpsuits, embellished with tassels, epaulettes, and a detachable six-pack. Names are emblazoned on the back of each one – Muvva, The Artist, Pitbull and Queenie. One of the actors, TerriAnn, addresses the audience,

> A little known fact for you, you know women's prisons in the UK don't actually ever have uniforms or jumpsuits?
> But we look good right? (Gregg et al., 2019: 55).

She winks at the audience and the audience laughs, complicit in the shared knowledge that images of women prisoners wearing orange jumpsuits are potent and heavily circulated thanks to the success of *Orange is the New Black*, Netflix's most watched, internationally syndicated series, set in the fictional Litchfield Penitentiary. Even if you have never watched the series, in all likelihood you know what it is and have a myriad of visual references to it.

The actors improvise a production meeting for a new television drama about women in prison. On the projection screen, slides of a story structure and TV-show formula are replaced by images and names of television series and films about women in prison: *Femmes in Prison, Women in Chains, Women in Cages, Escape from a Women's Prison*. Another actor, Jade, says:

> Okay so I know what you are thinking. You're thinking, 'Not another television show about women in prison.' Right?
> You've seen *Orange Is the New Black*. You've seen *Locked Up*. You've seen *Bad Girls* – the TV show and the musical. So what have we got that's different? Well, for one, we've all been to prison. We know what it's like. We

know what was funny, we know what was boring, we know what was sad. And we know what mum and dad sitting at home in front of a telly on a Saturday night want to see.

We've got the real shit, and trust me, it's dark as fuck, and it will knock your socks off.

[...]

TERRIANN: Also it's got a brilliant name. We're calling it
ALL: "Inside Bitch"

(Gregg et al., 2019: 69–71)

Inside Bitch (2019), in form and content, playfully and rigorously critiques the ubiquity of popular cultural representations of women in prison that are reductive but influential – women who are 'bad', 'monstrous' and, as the extensive repertoire of prison sexploitation film titles illustrates, objectified and sexualised. *Caged Heat* (1974), *Lust for Freedom* (1987) and *The Hot Box* (1972 are merely a snapshot of an expansive genre of film, with posters featuring naked or scantily clothed women, with by-lines including 'women so hot with desire they

Figure 7 *Inside Bitch* (2019), devised by Clean Break Members with Stacey Gregg and Deborah Pearson, Royal Court. Photographer: Niall McDiarmid

melt the chains that enslave them' (*The Big Bird Cage,* 1972). *Inside Bitch* – conceived by Stacey Gregg and Deborah Pearson and devised with Clean Break Members, Lucy Edkins, Jennifer Joseph, TerriAnn Oudjar and Jade Small – invites audiences to interrogate societal assumptions and wilful ignorance of the lived experience of criminalised women and the wider social implications of this.

Through a series of scenes – some scripted, some improvised around tasks, and all directly engaging with the audience – the cast's personal experiences of incarceration are interwoven through the play's overarching structure about developing a pitch for 'another television show about women in prison'. The result was a piece of theatre that, at times, provoked belly laughs from the audience and, at others, an uncomfortable silence: an acknowledgment of society's tolerance of and, indeed, its desire for, reductive and delimiting representations of women and prison; the negation of the lived experience of criminalised women; and an unquestioned acceptance of prison as a mode of state-sanctioned punishment.

Whilst the theatrical form of *Inside Bitch* (2019) marked a distinctive shift for the company, it is a continuation of Clean Break's sustained activist commitment to engaging publics with these issues through theatre, occasionally television[9] and, recently, radio.[10] In an interview given in 1980, Jacki Holborough said, 'We hope the plays will give people a better idea about what happens in prison and break down some of the misunderstandings that exist' (qtd in Palmer and Forlong, 1980). In the five decades since, Clean Break has continued to expose and critique these misunderstandings whilst also developing an expanded representational vocabulary for audiences, challenging them to think about the myths reiterated in society and the hard truths it refuses to engage with.

Drawing on social epistemology, epistemic injustice, criminology and carceral geography, we consider the ways that Clean Break expands epistemological understandings of criminalised women and carceral society. In short, how do we know what we know about criminalised women? How does Clean Break's theatre practice expose limited narratives about them and expand society's thinking to incorporate alternative ones?

---

[9] In the 1980s, Clean Break collaborated with Bob Long from Longshot Productions to develop a television adaptation of *Killers* (Channel 4, 1984) and the documentary, *Sex and Violence in Women's Prisons* (Channel 4, 1984); Gillian Mebarak's *Treading on my Tale* was directed by Maggie Ford for Channel 4 (1989).

[10] *Blis-ta* (2022) by Sonya Hale can be accessed at www.cleanbreak.org.uk/productions/blis-ta/ [accessed 23 March 2023].

3.1 Presumption ... and Other Narrative Possibilities

In order to analyse how Clean Break does this, we need to take a step back to think about how information is constructed and circulated: What do we know about criminalised women? How does this knowledge get made and circulated? Why does it matter?

In the introduction to *Criminal Women* (1985), Carlen writes,

> To the present-day reader the early theories of female criminality appear at their most benign to be faintly comical; at their most malignant to be blatantly sexist. [...] Lombroso and Ferrero's book *The Female Offender* published in 1895 contained most of the stereotypical elements responsible for subsequent characterizations of women lawbreakers. [In it] [...] are all the elements of a penology for women which persists, right up to the present time, in constituting women criminals as being both within and without femininity, criminality, adulthood and sanity. These misogynous themes not only occur again and again in the theories of women's crime but what is more important, they continue to have a tenacious hold upon the minds of judges, magistrates and the administrators of women's prisons. (1985: 1–3)

And, we would argue, a general public. Carlen's comments, written nearly four decades ago, continue to be pertinent and, as *Inside Bitch* so persuasively reminds us, these assumptions, myths, and stereotypes about criminalised women continue to infiltrate the popular imagination through news, documentaries, word of mouth and, particularly, cultural representations in film and TV. The power of cultural representation as a system of knowledge transmission about crime, criminals and punishment is recognised by cultural criminologists, and explicitly by popular criminologists, Nicole Rafter and Michelle Brown when they write, 'criminology is hard at work in culture and that culture is hard at work in criminology' (2011: 1).

There is a growing body of academic work in popular criminology considering film, television, and literature, particularly novels (Bailey and Hale, 1997; Rafter and Brown, 2011) but there is limited consideration, to date, of theatre and performances' contribution to criminological discourse and knowledge creation. Whilst films, television and literature operate within an economy of circulation that allows for limitless audiences and the infinite circulation of ideas, narratives and images through repeat viewing and reading, the ontology of theatre and performance necessitates a time-limited, live interaction with specific audiences. But although theatre operates with different modes and economies of audience, it is important not to dismiss or underestimate its power in developing new epistemological understandings. Performance scholar Aylwyn Walsh, drawing cultural criminology to bear on theatre studies, asserts 'the importance of performance in constituting the carceral imaginary. Its significance is its concern with the body in relation to spectatorship and meaning making as valuable when understood against and through how crime and punishment are scripted, enacted and received' (2019: 5).

In this section, we consider some of the ways that Clean Break's attention to women's experiences of criminalisation develops new understandings about prison as a fabrication of social control and power relations in carceral society. Our analysis is built upon two key ideas about the creation and circulation of knowledge: social epistemology and epistemic injustice.

3.2 Not Presuming to Always Already Know

Social epistemology is 'the interdisciplinary inquiry into the myriad ways humans socially acquire, create, construct, transmit, store, represent, revise, and review knowledge, information, belief and judgement' (Fricker et al., 2019: xvii). In short, how do humans know things? Goldman proposes that knowledge is held and circulated in three main ways: how individuals acquire knowledge from others (interpersonal social epistemology); how groups may acquire knowledge (collective social epistemology) and how institutions acquire knowledge (institutional social epistemology) (2019: 10–20). Fricker et al. qualify this when they make explicit that 'institutions [...] themselves may not have beliefs, but are made of individuals or groups that do, [which] influence the creation and transmission of knowledge' (2019: xvii).

Since its inception, Clean Break has been concerned with the kinds of knowledge about women's experiences in circulation with individuals, groups, and institutions – particularly those within the criminal justice system. Theatre, with audiences of individuals gathered together as a group, offers opportunities for the development of interpersonal and collective social epistemology. The company's commitment to enhancing institutional social epistemology through touring work to prisons and training events for magistrates, police, probation services and policy makers has been evident from the very beginning: in 1979, when performing in Edinburgh for the first time, the company were invited to HMP Barlinnie, Glasgow, where they performed in the Special Unit, a small therapeutic community for violent men. Holborough's letter to Susan McCormick gives an insight into the impact of this for both the company and the audience:

> Barlinnie show including an MP and a female AG [Assistant Governor] [...] and Giles Havergill who is director of the much praised Glasgow Citizen's Theatre. [...] The discussion after, instead of the usual "What's it like to be in ", began with a "What's it like to be out?" [...] The visit affected the group with

a conflict of emotions but made us keen to try and perform in other prisons. (Holborough, 1979d)

The following year, Clean Break's tour schedule for *In or Out* (Hicks and Mottley) and *Killers* (Holborough) details performances in theatres, colleges, health settings (London Hospital and Maudsley Hospital, London) as well as criminal justice settings including a return to Edinburgh Festival and Barlinnie's Special Unit; Pucklechurch Remand Centre, Bristol; Inner London Probation Service; and a Prison Psychologists Conference.

Since the 1980s, the criminologist Pat Carlen has significantly influenced thinking about formal and informal social control on women's experiences, particularly criminalisation and incarceration. Carlen listened to incarcerated women, recognising their expertise in their own lives, articulating how the 'processes and practices of social control and regulation shape the lives, subjectivities and worlds of the powerless [...] and to what effect' (Phoenix, 2012: 258). She was a major influence on Clean Break's thinking about the personal and political implications of criminalisation and incarceration in a capitalist social order. The book *Criminal Women* (1985), edited by Carlen, focused on the narratives of four women who had been sentenced for criminal offences. Three of them – Jenny Hicks, Josie O'Dwyer and Chris Tchaikovsky – were Members of Clean Break in the early and mid-1980s and Carlen collaborated

Figure 8 Jenny Hicks and Eva Mottley *In or Out (1981) by Jenny Hicks, Oval House Theatre*

Figure 9 Jacki Holborough and Cat Coull *Killers* (1981) by Jacki Holborough, Edinburgh Fringe Festival

with Chris Tchaikovsky to establish, in 1983, the campaigning organisation Women in Prison, which continues today. One of the most important ideas in thinking about the ways in which Clean Break's theatre practices can expand the epistemological landscape, is Carlen's concept of the 'criminological imagination'. This is an acknowledgement of the duality of the processes and practices of social control alongside the possibility that 'the ordering of things can always be otherwise' (2012: 345). For Carlen, Clean Break and Women in Prison, the duality of how things are *and* the criminological imagination in envisioning that 'the ordering of things can always be otherwise' is an activist imperative, fundamental to any kind of personal, social and political change. For Clean Break, theatre was a collaborative, creative and critical act of imagination with other women who had personal experience of prison and with audiences who had none.

Carlen's caution, 'while prisons do exist we must never presume that we always already know what goes on behind the walls' (Carlen, 1983: 218), is pertinent to thinking about women's experiences of incarceration: while women in prisons do exist we must never presume that we always already know who they are or what their experiences are behind the walls. Clean Break's creation of over 100 plays, informed by women's often hidden or unacknowledged experiences, is an extraordinary epistemological resource that directly intervenes in epistemic injustice (Fricker, 2010).

3.3 Testimonial Injustice

Miranda Fricker's work on epistemic injustice (2010, 2016) offers productive ways for us to analyse Clean Break's work as social epistemological practices through three lenses: 'testimonial injustice', hermeneutical injustice and 'the preservation of ignorance'. Fricker argues that 'testimonial injustice' happens when someone is not believed because of assumptions and prejudice about who they are: 'An example [...] might be that the police do not believe you because you are black' (2010: 1). Testimonial injustice occurs when 'the level of credibility attributed to a speaker's word is reduced by prejudice operative in the hearer's judgement' (2016: 161). Feminist criminologists, penal historians and reformers have evidenced how, time and again, the testimony of women in police custody, courts of law and the court of public opinion is belittled and dismissed because of assumptions and prejudice about women generally and specifically women who have been accused of committing a crime who, as sociological data continues to evidence, have life experiences shaped by societal disadvantage in relation to race, class, health, education and poverty (Agozino, 1997; Kennedy, 1993, 2018; McCorkel, 2013). In these contexts, criminalised women's capacity as 'knowers' is undermined or derided because of prejudice.

Clean Break directly addressed and redressed this testimonial injustice. From its inception, the company boldly declared and aligned the company's identity as its authority to speak about women's experience of criminalisation through personal experience: 'Clean Break Women's Theatre Group' (Hicks and Holborough, 1979), 'Clean Break Women Prisoners Theatre' (Clean Break, 1979) and 'Clean Break Theatre Group (Women Prisoners)' and a 'successful theatre group made up of women ex-prisoners' (Clean Break, 1982).

Women
Prisoners
Ex-Prisoners
Theatre

These referents are defiant declarations of expertise without a whisper of apology, shame or stigma – no matter what wider society may assume to know, think or judge about women, women prisoners and women ex-prisoners. Or, for that matter, women who make theatre.

All of the work created during the first decade of the company's life was written, devised and performed by women with experience of the criminal justice system. Some of the earlier plays, particularly *Killers* (1980) and *Decade* (1984), are explicit about the material conditions of women's incarceration and the wider social apathy and political neglect that shapes this. Both *Killers* (Holborough, 1980) and *Decade* (Holborough, 1984) were located in H-wing, a maximum-security unit which held women within HMP Durham. This notorious unit, called E-Wing, was originally built for twenty-five men, convicted of acts of violence, who posed a serious threat to society. The conditions were inhumane and, after hunger strikes and riots by the men which drew enough public concern to warrant political action, the prison was closed in 1971. Four years later it was reopened as women's unit. Of the thirty-five women held in the renamed H-Wing, three were Category A prisoners, convicted of acts of terrorism and murder. The other thirty-two women were given short sentences for non-violent crimes such as theft and fraud – they were the 'day trippers' (Holborough, 1984: 11). *Killers* explicitly and succinctly summarises the shifts in prison practices: 'When the men were here there were protests. Demonstrations every day'.

> Hunger strikes, mutinies, escape attempts. Questions in the house. The media waited eagerly for news of fresh disturbance from Durham's E-wing. Committees of experts came and went filing reports about psychological damage and conditions intolerable to civilised society. So they moved the men out. And after a decent lapse of time and a change of title, they moved the women in. Since which time the wing has hardly been known to exist. There are only women here now. Tension is all premenstrual. Give 'em enough Valium and they'll fade from view. (Holborough, 1980d: 11).

The phrases 'hardly been known to exist' and 'they'll fade from view' are indicative of the social and political neglect of incarcerated women prevalent in the late 1970s and, as Clean Break's work continues to illustrate, endures. In *Decade,* the character of Jane – an incarcerated women in a high security prison – crystallises the differentiated view of the representation of men and women in news and public discourse, 'Christ, men go on hunger strike or in solitary, women diet and stay in their rooms' (Holborough, 1984: 34). She also recounts how this is symptomatic of a system which has historically gendered the criminological subject as male: If I were a man there'd be a dozen dispersal units to shunt me around but as a woman I'm just a token. A freak. Caged up in this tiny space in the middle of a man's prison because I'm all there is' (Holborough, 1984: 13). 'The whole thing is designed to keep us gagged and in our place. [...] We're only women. We don't riot because then they'd set the men on us – and the dogs. [...] I could start a revolution in the bog but mention solidarity and the subject is changed to parole dates. They've got too much to lose' (Holborough, 1984: 11).

'H' wing was a single unit for women within a larger male prison complex – 'a tomb', 'a concrete submarine', 'a prison within a prison: buried in the middle of larger building housing 1000 men' (Holborough, 1980d: 1). All of the women in 'H' wing were subject to the maximum-security prison conditions, where cell doors were secured with, 'Not one, not two but three sets of bars at my bullet-proof window. Looking onto the fences, the wall, the camera, the scanner lights, barbed wire, dogs' (Holborough, 1980d: 15). At the time, there were local campaigns (led by Women in Durham Prison Support Group) and a national campaign (led by Women in Prison) to bring attention to the oppressive 'living conditions and measures imposed in the name of security' which prompted the Howard League for Penal Reform to recommend its closure (1979). Both *Killers* and *Decade* contributed to this campaign of public understanding through fictional narratives, based on women's life experiences, alongside articles such as, 'Like Living in a Submarine', that appeared in the Radical Alternatives to Prison magazine, *The Abolitionist* (Hicks and Boyle, 1983: 3). Through performance and alternative publications, women's experiences in Durham H Wing therefore circulated more widely than before.

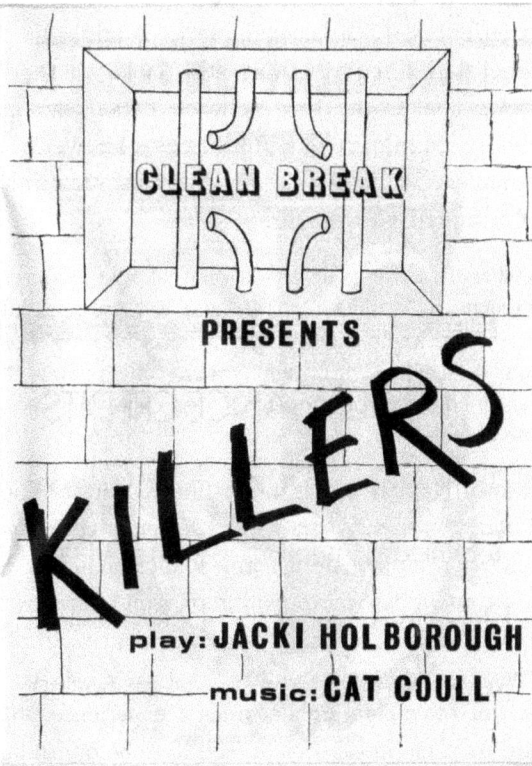

Figure 10 *Killers* (1980), Pleasance Theatre Programme, Edinburgh Fringe

Fricker states that 'An epistemic system characterised by testimonial injustice is a system in which ignorance will repeatedly prevail over potentially shared knowledge, despite speakers' best efforts' (2016: 162). As the following reviews show, Clean Break's theatre practice directly intervened in the epistemic system as an act of redress. Their authority and credibility are recognised and valued:

> The actors do give the impression that they have lived their material and that [...] they know what they're talking and acting about (Ross, *The Scotsman*, 1981).

> Outstanding insight into what leads women to prison by those who should know. Compulsive (Critics' Choice, *Edinburgh Evening News*, 1981)

3.4 Hermeneutical injustice

Hermeneutical injustice occurs, Fricker argues, when society does not know about, recognise, or have the vocabulary to talk about something. She calls this 'a gap in collective interpretative resources' that 'puts someone at an unfair disadvantage when it comes to making sense of their social experiences; [...] an example [...] might be that you suffer sexual harassment in a culture that still lacks that critical concept' (2010: 1). Fricker makes the link between those who may experience testimonial injustice (diminished credibility as a knower because of prejudice, e.g. criminalised women) and with hermeneutical injustice (e.g. the experiences of criminalised women):

> Being a member of a social group that does not contribute on an equal footing with other groups to that shared interpretative resource [...] puts one at an unfairly increased risk of having social experiences that one needs, perhaps urgently, to understand and/or communicate to certain powerful others – to a teacher, an employer, a police officer, a jury – but which cannot be made mutual sense of in the shared terms available. (2016: 163)

If representations of women in prison are limited and lacking in the nuance which reflects lived experience, the gap in society's collective interpretative resources continues to perpetuate a hermeneutical injustice not just against them, but also their families, the organisations, and networks which seek to support them and, ultimately, society. It reinscribes and reiterates the violence of structural disadvantage and social control.

Clean Break not only highlights women's experience within prison but carefully attends to the circumstances of their lives before and the implications for their lives after. The press materials for a tour of *Avenues* in Merseyside

(1981) explain that it is a play about three women, written by members of the cast and 'based on real experiences':

> Mary – and how she comes to commit a crime.
> Debbie – and how she is dealt with by family and the law after arrest for mugging.
> Kathy – and how she is dealt with in prison after being sentenced for a crime she didn't commit. (Holborough et al., 1981)

Avenues offers a simple, structural premise, however reviewers at the time articulate how the play's nuanced understandings about women's experiences within the criminal justice system provide, in Fricker's words, interpretative resources to talk about these experiences:

> "Avenues" is an intense and refreshing look at an institution that the vast majority of the population will never experience but nevertheless should consider. (LT Edinburgh Evening News, 1981.)

> The production simply highlights the widening gap between fixed rules and the human situations to which they are meant to apply. Neither morbid, nor full of false hope, *Avenues* is part of Clean Break's exposé of the way women are being dealt with by a system which is irrelevant and uncaring of their situation. (*Spare Rib*, Oct 1981)

> Clean Break (Women Prisoners' Theatre) present a show which is not agit-prop and which avoids any crude didacticism. The audience are left to make their own connections between the three stories and draw their own conclusions [...] Although *Avenues* is based on "real-life" situations, it does not consist of slices of raw life served up as art. It implicitly questions how Law Courts mete out their justice and how solicitors and social workers function in relation to that justice, and it quietly but firmly reveals the emotional and social complexities which can lie behind even the most petit (sic) crime. (Ross, *The Scotsman*, 1981)

We have quoted from the reviews at length because they evidence the ways in which Clean Break engages with the possibilities of theatre making to do something other than report, document or didactically denounce. Instead, Clean Break creates spaces for the audiences to think rather than be told, 'to make their own connections', to 'draw their own conclusions'. This creation of narrative and representational frameworks offers shared points of reference for critical engagement and, as accounts of the after-show discussions evidence, invigorated discussion. Jacki Holborough's letter to Susan McCormick offers a textured sense of this engagement and questioning:

> JACKON'S LANE. [...] The group had excited a great deal of interest and people were keen to talk. [...] Some wanted to know what were our

individual reasons for being in prison in the first place. We avoided opening up discussion on that level, preferring to stick to broader issues. A lot of people agreed that the great value was in seeing prisoners as ordinary 'nice' people: in being able to relate in a relaxed way to this section of society usually 'hidden' and realising that there seems to be no great difference between 'them' and the 'us' of it all. There was a feeling that what we were doing was in some way unique. One or two people had come armed with statistics and what sounded like ready-made (RAP) [Radical Alternatives to Prison] lectures. It was all very friendly though, and the applause was hefty when we eventually left the stage. People obviously wanted to go on talking since while Krissie and I were picking up bits of costume and props afterwards, half the audience seemed to converge on us with further questions and theories. (1979c)

In 1989, there was a seismic change in the way that Clean Break developed new plays. As the organisation moved from a collective to a more traditional model of hierarchical theatre management with funding and business plans, Clean Break employed women who were sympathetic to the mission of the company rather than women who had personal experience of incarceration. There was a fundamental shift away from the representation of women with lived experience in the decision-making processes of the company *and* in the theatre work produced. Until this point, the creation of plays by women who had experience of prison was prioritised – their experience, authenticity and authority were integral to the identity of the company. The production of Bryony Lavery's *Wicked* (1990) was the first in a new phase of the company's commissioning practices, where professional writers wrote plays informed by their research about women's experience of the criminal justice system. Whilst this decision prompted ongoing debate and reflection within the organisation for the next three decades, it meant that the company produced work that represented a wider terrain of women's experiences – both in terms of what those experiences were and the range of theatre forms employed to engage audiences.

The company's relentless commitment to expose the hidden narratives beyond the stereotypes of women and crime, details an expansive and interconnected range of social injustices including: racism (*24%*, 1991, Paulette Randall); mental illness (*Sounds Like an Insult*, 2014, Vivienne Franzmann); enduring poverty and social immobility (*Spent*, 2016, Katherine Chandler); addiction (*Pests* 2014, Vivienne Franzmann); family rupture (*Apatche Tears*, 2000, Lin Coghlan; *Billy the Girl*, 2013, Katy Hims); the impact of faith in relation to intergenerational shame (*House*, 2016, Somalia Seaton; *Favour*, 2022, Ambreen Razia); the particularity of friendships forged between women when serving sentences together (*Little on the Inside*, 2013, Alice Birch; *This Wide* Night, 2008, Chloë Moss); and sex trafficking and illegal

Figure 11 WICKED *Wicked* (1990) by Bryony Lavery, Oval Theatre. Photographer Sarah Ainslie

immigration (*it felt empty when the heart left but it's alright now*, 2009, Lucy Kirkwood). This brief selection of plays illustrates some of the ways that Clean Break has invited publics to attend to the experience of women whose lives are often masked by stereotype and lazy cultural representation. They detail hidden backstories that shape individual women's experiences, reminding audiences, echoing Carlen, to not presume to always already know the detail of someone's life. They address hermeneutic injustices by providing collective interpretative resources for society to see, understand and respond to.

3.5 Narrative Discomfort, 'the preservation of ignorance', and *[BLANK]*

The company dared to speak out about their experiences as women at a particular historical moment and detail through a growing catalogue of plays, the influence of informal social control (patriarchal values which position women in the domestic, feminine sphere as normal and anything other as deviant) and formal social control (the ways in which the criminal justice system neglects the specific needs of women within its care, layering additional punishment on the sanctioned removal of liberty). It would be easier and understandable if the anger and pain of this experience led women to a place of blame and condemnation, of further social segregation as an act of self-protection. However, Clean Break, acknowledging social fear and political apathy, stepped towards others, offering their experience as a bridge to new knowledge and understanding about the current state of play and the knowledge that things could be different. This duality is what Carlen refers to as the 'criminological imagination'. Imagination is the key word here; to imagine is a creative act, it is to create an expanded sense of possibilities, of ways of being. But this takes collaboration – between Clean Break as theatre makers and audiences as collaborators. And this is where Miranda Fricker's and Gaile Pohlhaus Jnr's work on the preservation of ignorance is pertinent. Wilful ignorance

> occurs when dominantly situated knowers refuse to acknowledge epistemic tools developed from the experienced world of those situated marginally. Such refusals allow dominantly situated knowers to misunderstand, misinterpret, and/or ignore whole parts of the world. (Pohlhaus, 2012: 715)

Since the 1970s, there have been a number of damning reports about the conditions of women's imprisonment in the UK (Corston, 2007; Owers, 2005; Ramsbotham, 1997). At the point of each publication there is outrage, followed by the declaration of political promises which, after a period of time in which next to nothing happens, the mumbling of political excuses follows. When the male prisoners at HMP Durham's E wing protested conditions, the unit closed within a few years. When the women in the renamed H Wing protested and prison ombudsman reports condemned it as oppressive and not fit for habitation, it took 30 years before the unit was closed. In 2006, the deaths of six women over thirteen months in HMP Styal was the tragic catalyst for a government review of the treatment of vulnerable women in the criminal justice system. This was led by Jean Corston and in her report (2007), she contextualised the ongoing, wilful neglect:

> I have been dismayed at the high prevalence of institutional misunderstanding within the criminal justice system of the things that matter to women and at the shocking level of unmet need. Yet the compelling body of research which has accumulated over many years consistently points to remedies. Much of this research was commissioned by government. There can be few topics that have been so exhaustively researched to such little practical effect as the plight of women in the criminal justice system (2007: 16).

Corston's report detailed forty-three explicit recommendations to address failures and gaps in the system. When it was published, it was welcomed as both an exposition of successive governments' scandalous neglect and a blueprint for structural change. More than a decade later, community-based initiatives to support vulnerable women that were outlined in Corston's report have been decimated by government cuts undertaken in the name of austerity. In 2017, to mark a decade since the publication of the report with a clear and feasible action plan, Women in Prison, the charity established by Carlen and Tchaikovsky, detailed the minimal amount of action taken. This lack of action and 'preservation of ignorance' is motivated or 'wilful' (Pohlhaus, 2012).

To consider how Clean Break has explicitly noted the implications of such ignorance, we conclude Section 3 with analysis of Alice Birch's *[BLANK]*. As we shall demonstrate, the play, through form, content, and curation of scenes from the text, makes an important contribution to understandings about criminalised women and the long shadows of stigma and shame that haunt and shape their lives. [*BLANK*] is a prompt to 'see' and 'hear' – to engage with the lives and voices of women too often banished behind the material bricks and mortar of prison walls and the ethereal but all too concrete cultural representations of stereotype, that fix social understandings about women, crime, and punishment.

[BLANK], was co-commissioned by Clean Break and the Donmar Warehouse as part of Clean Break's fortieth anniversary celebrations. Within the Clean Break repertoire, the play had an usually large cast of potentially fourteen children, young people and adults. It also offered a distinctive form –

Figure 12 Rehearsal of *[BLANK]* (2019) by Alice Birch, Donmar Warehouse. Photographer: Helen Maybanks

100 possible scenes – to engage both theatre makers and audiences in the politics of witnessing representations of criminalised women on stage and the consequences of this off stage. Birch offers some rules to guide a theatre company navigating this text:

> This play is a challenge and an invitation to you and your company to make your own play from these scenes. [...] The play consists of 100 scenes in total Scenes 1–45 are for children. Scenes 46–55 are for adults and children. Scenes 56–100 are for adults. You and your company can choose as many or as few scenes as you like. You may present them in any order you like. You may repeat scenes. (2019, n.p)

With the Donmar production, Maria Aberg, the director, led the selection of twenty-two of the scenes. The characters are identified as A, B, C etc. Some scenes feature one character, some two or three, and Scene 100, an epic dinner party scene features fourteen characters. The people we meet in one scene, may or may not appear in another.

If you read the text in its entirety, you get snapshots of lives, already ruptured by events that have happened off stage, some potentially years ago, some recently. A child on the phone to its mother, anxious that it took seven rings for her to pick up, keen to know if she's taken her medication, if she's paid the bills, who she's with, to tell them she loves them – again, and again, and again, and again, and again, and again (Scene 7 – Seven). A mother who catches her daughter breaking into the family home in the middle of the night to find money or goods to sell to pay for drugs; who refuses to 'help' her daughter by giving her money, whose daughter says that if she doesn't, she'll have to go and get money another way – prostitution (Scene 54 – Cry). A mother, potentially, the same one, in conversation with a young, nervous police officer who has come to tell her that her daughter has been found dead (Scene 66 – Transference). A mother making 'posh' pizza for her daughter who is concerned that, for her mother, getting her head stamped in, is all in a day's work when dealing with perpetrators of domestic violence (Scene 8 – Pizza). A child who has recently arrived in a care home, opens a letter from their mother who is in prison, and finds a mix tape she has made. This is calmly and slowly unspooled by another child as part of an extraordinarily short, slow but vicious exposition of their power (Scene 4 – Tape). Of a group of children, who have created t-shirts and a Facebook page as part of a search party to look for someone's mum – who has gone missing eight times before (Scene 5 – T-Shirts). A pregnant woman in a prison cell who has just been told that she's been accepted into a mother and baby unit – who is torn between accepting this or turning it down because the unit is even further away from her children than the prison, who worries that:

> They have never felt Chosen. So. By me. I think, They will feel. Find this Hard. Think that I've perhaps. Chosen Not Them. Again. And I'm. I..I thought. If I Applied then I'm doing my best by This baby. But that I wouldn't get in, And then nothing would be different for my other ones. The ones at. At. Home. (254–255)

[BLANK]'s patchwork of characters and narratives offers an extraordinary range of representations of lives shaped by societal structures of disadvantage which are in one way or another in contact with the criminal justice system. In a context where women with experience of the criminal justice system are too often dismissed as unreliable or untrustworthy, *[BLANK]* invites us to consider who and what is made visible and who and what is invisible; to examine the stories we choose to engage with, the voices we choose to listen to. Whilst fictional accounts about women affected by the criminal justice system in popular television series or films may have a clear beginning, middle and end, the reality is very different, refusing to be contained within a single, neat narrative frame. *[BLANK]* – Alice Birch's invitation to choose from 100 possible scenes, to play with their order and staging – is a call to considered action. But the choice to take action – to see, to hear, to witness, to intervene in narratives about women's criminalisation which reiterate epistemic injustice – lies with the audience.

Birch makes this explicit in Scene 100 – Dinner Party – which has a cast of 14 featuring a head-teacher, a lawyer, a therapist, an architect, and a BAFTA winning documentary film maker who makes women-centred work that is 'very Dynamic. Very authored. Full of movement. Aesthetically engaged' (474). They indulge in a feast of labneh, fattoush and pomegranate dip, whilst snorting the cocaine delivered by the courier who has brought along her holiday cover so she can learn the route. In the midst of this seemingly socially aware group, the new girlfriend of A, who may or may not have had an abusive mother, interrupts saying:

> I think you Say the right fucking things to one another. I think you Observe and Consume and Nourish yourselves with as much of the Awful as you can possibly stomach each day, in order to buy yourself the time and the life to do absolutely nothing of worth or meaning or good in the world. I think you will spend your whole lives making no change. Living in your bubbles. Patting one another on the back. Crying for people rather than condemning. Failing to either Listen or have a Complex conversation and Learn. I think you are making the world worse. Every fucking day (515)

This failure to 'Listen or have a Complex conversation and Learn', despite having access to information and knowledge that could genuinely impact social and cultural understandings about criminalised women, is, in Fricker's words –

'the preservation of ignorance'; an investment in the status quo where capitalist social order is maintained through a seeming to hear and care rather than actually hearing and caring. Without it, there will be no understanding, there will be no reform. This sentiment reflects the words of Jennifer Joseph, an actor from *Inside Bitch,* during a post-show discussion,

> We've been talking. It's just not today and yesterday. The talking's been talked even before I went to jail. But who's listening? The people that have been in charge, that can do something about it, if they're not listening, we're just wasting our time. [...] All this talking ain't doing nothing. Someone needs to be listening otherwise what's the point. (Joseph, 2019)

With *[BLANK]*, Birch offers readers, theatre makers and audiences an opportunity to, echoing Jennifer, listen: to realise a radical ambition for theatre to attend to and witness the complexity of the lives of criminalised women; to invigorate understandings about how they are enmeshed in intersectional inequality and violence within wider societal structures of disadvantage.

Clean Break exposes the mechanisms of carceral society through its attention to the lives of criminalised women. For more than 40 years it has developed different organisational and artistic strategies in its commitment to new epistemological understandings about prison as a material and ideological fabrication of power relations in carceral society and, specifically, the experiences of criminalised women shaped by them.

Each of Clean Break's plays offers a provocation to audiences to examine what we expect of narratives of criminalised women, why we expect them and how our understandings can fracture or re-iterate the social structures which continue to impact a life too often marked by stigma and shame. We argue that Clean Break's work is an act of feminist social epistemology, with theatre practices expanding audiences' 'knowledge, information, belief and judgement' (Fricker et al., 2019: xvii) about women and criminalisation. But it's a dialogic process. Clean Break can make theatre, it can tour to a wide range of audiences, it can create spaces for dialogue, but it is up to individuals who make up groups, institutions, and society to do the creative, critical work of criminological imagining too.

An unwillingness to care enough to understand leads to what Duakas (2019) refers to as epistemic marginalization, a kind of epistemic injustice which will 'distort the social-epistemic landscape so that knowledge and other epistemic goods do not flow as they should' (Fricker et al., 2019: xx). Clean Break's work not only identifies this distortion but un-fixes the anchors of limited representation and epistemic injustice. The plays become new representational coordinates to navigate popular understanding and knowledge about women, crime, and justice. Holborough's comment made in 1981 rings as true now and it did then (qtd in Palmer and Forlong, 1981):

> We're not trying to push a message [...] We're trying to communicate, to share our experiences. We're trying to make people remember that while they're actually watching us on stage there are women locked away.

Conclusion

In the late nineteenth century, Kentish Town (London) was the epicentre of the UK's piano and organ-making industry. This was in part due to its location on the canal enabling these heavy instruments to be transported more easily, shipped out on the canals of north London, around the country and across the world. It was a thriving industry with over a hundred piano makers operating in the area, which held specialist craft and creative knowledge. That industry has now disappeared, but in its place is another hub of specialist knowledge. Down one of Kentish Town's cobbled alleyways, where there used to be an old piano factory, there now stands a building that is 'bright, soft, open and honest' (Avanti, 1995) where women come together and share their craft to collectively produce beautiful, joyful, and heavy creative work. This work is held, shaped, and built in Kentish Town but travels all over the UK and, sometimes, internationally. Over forty years after its founding at HMP Askham Grange, Clean Break continue to offer training and create theatre at this base and also tour projects and performances to prisons, theatres and third sector organisations.

Across this Element we have explored Clean Break Theatre's origins and practices by offering the first extended historiography of the company's emergence; mapping the modalities of endurance that are embedded within the education programme; and asserting the ways in which its performance work expands epistemological understandings of criminalised women. Our engagement with the formation of the company proposes the need for greater attention to how arts company founding narratives might be deployed to different political or artistic ends in particular cultural moments and policy landscapes. This Element also undertakes the first extended and holistic engagement with Clean Break's education programme. By foregrounding endurance in our analysis of this strand of the company's work we have offered a critical framework through which to read the survival of the company, persistence of its practice, and attention to the everyday, often imperceptible harms women in the criminal justice system encounter. Finally, we have underscored how Clean Break's performance practice illuminates the mechanisms of carceral society. Beyond simply representing these mechanisms, the company intervenes in hegemonic understandings of justice.

Through its artistic practice it offers new epistemological understandings about carceral society and the structures of power that it maintains.

Located in a series on Women Theatre Makers, this Element exploring the work of Clean Break, illuminates a significant body of women playwrights, performers, directors, technicians, designers, educators and facilitators. The company has commissioned over 100 original plays which expose women's experiences of structural inequality and violence through criminalisation and incarceration. Its work has been performed in a range of venues: from established theatre spaces to sites which aim to engage a wider range of audiences – such as probation training events, mental health conferences and the Ministry of Justice. We have tried to document as wide a range of work and creatives as possible in these pages, but the thousands of women theatre makers who have passed through Clean Break are impossible to fully capture. What is evident across these pages is the persistence of women theatre makers in the face of the patriarchal architectures of carceral society; the richness of women stories, as illuminated by the company's own narratives and the narratives it stages; and the resourcefulness of the shifting collective of women theatre makers involved in the company across its five decades.

When asked by a current Clean Break Member about her dreams for the company's future, founding member Jenny Hicks reflected, 'I don't think it's for me to hope now, it's for you to hope. Tell me what you want'. (Hicks, 2019). This is indicative of the now intergenerational nature of Clean Break: its longevity is sustained by the successive waves of women passing through its doors, with the company being held by different generations that have collectively imagined what Clean Break might be or what it might become. Through engaging with archival material, interviews, and the company's performance work across its over forty-year history, we have been able to trace the threads that stretch across these decades of work. While there have been different people, organisational structures, cultural and policy landscapes across this period, throughout their existence Clean Break have maintained a commitment to hope, the kind of hope that both provides a sanctuary and also fights for a different future. It is now for us, for you, for we to hope for what the future of Clean Break might be and to join them in demanding the reforms we need in our justice systems.

References

Agozino, Biko (1997) *Black Women and the Criminal Justice System: Toward the Decolonisation of Victimisation*, Abingdon: Routledge.

Amanquah, Sylvia (2020) Interview with Clean Break Archive Project and Women Theatre Justice Research Team. London, 21 February.

Avanti Architects (1995) Feasibility Study for the Development of 2 Patshull Road, London NW5 As a New Training Centre, Unpublished document. Clean Break archive.

Ashby, Imogen and Franzmann, Vivienne (2020) Interview with Clean Break Archive Project and Women Theatre Justice Research Team. London, 31 January.

Aston, Elaine (1995) *An Introduction to Feminism and Theatre*, London: Routledge.

Aston, Elaine (2003) *Feminist Views on the English Stage: Women Playwrights 1990–2000*, Cambridge: Cambridge University Press.

Ashton, Zawe (2010) *She from the Sea*. Unpublished play text, Clean Break archives, Bishopsgate, London.

Bailey, Frankie Y., and Hale, Donna C. (1997) *Popular Culture, Crime, and Justice*, United Kingdom: Wadsworth.

Bartley, Sarah (2019) 'Gendering Welfare: Acts of Reproductive Labour in Applied Performance Practice', *Contemporary Theatre Review*, 29.3, 305–319.

Bartley, Sarah (2021) '"How We Open the Doors to a Community": Creative Collaborations and Aesthetic Strategies in Social Isolation' in L. Bissel and L. Weir (eds.), *Performance in a Pandemic*, London: Routledge, 79–86.

Bartley, Sarah (2022) 'What Transformative Justice Looks Like: Developing Young Companies and Training Emerging Practitioners in Prison Arts Practice', in K. Freebody, C. Rajendra and S. Busby (eds.), *Routledge Companion on Theatre and Youth*, London: Routledge.

Birch, Alice (2013) *Little on the Inside*, unpublished play text, London: Clean Break.

Birch, Alice (2018) *[BLANK]*, London: Oberon.

Brady, Michael and Fricker, Miranda (2016) *The Epistemic Life of Groups: Essays in the Epistemology of Collectives*, Oxford: Oxford University Press.

Bradshaw, Sarah (2002) *Gendered Poverties and Power Relations: Looking Inside Communities and Households*, Managua: ICD, Embajada de Holanda, Puntos de Encuentro.

Brown, Michelle (2009) *The Culture of Punishment: Prison, Society, and Spectacle*, New York: New York University Press.

Brown, Michelle (2013) 'Penal Spectatorship and the Culture of Punishment' in D. Scott (ed.), *Why Prison? Cambridge Studies in Law and Society*, Cambridge: Cambridge University Press, 108–124.

Bruce, Deborah (2016) *Hear*, unpublished play text, London: Clean Break.

Bruce, Deborah (2023) *Dixon and Daughters*, London: Nick Hern Books.

Bruce, Deborah, Ikoko, Theresa, Lomas, Laura, Odimba, Chino and Sarma, Ursula Rani (2015) *Joanne*, London: Nick Hern Books.

Busby, Selina and Abraham, Nicola (2015) 'Celebrating Success: How Has Participation in Clean Break's Theatre Education Programme Contributed to Individuals' Involvement in Professional or Community Arts Practices?', Project Report, The Royal Central School of Speech and Drama, London.

Cadogan, Peaches (2020) Interview with Clean Break archive project and Women Theatre Justice research team. London, 21 February.

Carlen, Pat (1983) *Women's Imprisonment: A Study in Social Control*, London: Routledge.

Carlen, Pat (1985) *Criminal Women: Autobiographical Accounts – Diana Christina, Jenny Hicks, Josie O' Dwyer, Chris Tchaikovsky and Pat Carlen*, Cambridge: Polity Press.

Carlen, Pat (2019) *A Criminological Imagination: Essays on Justice, Punishment, Discourse*. London: Routledge.

Chandler, Katherine (2016) *Spent*, unpublished play text, London: Clean Break.

Clarke, Rebecca and Williams, Patrick (2005). 'Women and Anger Programme Evaluation', *Reclaim North West*. https://artsevidence.org.uk/evaluations/women-and-anger/

Clean Break (1980) Marketing Material for tour of *In or Out? & Killers*, Clean Break archive, Bishopsgate, London.

Clean Break (1982) *Avenues* Programme, Clean Break archive, Bishopsgate, London.

Clean Break (1986) *The Sin Eaters* programme, Clean Break archive, Bishopsgate, London.

Clean Break (1989) 'Clean Break 1979–1989: 10 Years of Making the Break', Clean Break archive, Bishopsgate, London.

Clean Break (1992a) Clean Break Theatre Company Annual Report, https://register-of-charities.charitycommission.gov.uk/charity-search/-/charity-details/1017560/full-print. [accessed 1 December 2022].

Clean Break (1992) *Head-rot Holiday* Production Programme, Clean Break archive, Bishopsgate, London.

Clean Break (1992) Management Committee meeting notes, 14 May 1992, Clean Break archive, Bishopsgate, London.

Clean Break (1995) Management Committee meeting notes, 1 June 1995, Clean Break archive, Bishopsgate, London.

Clean Break (1995). Training Programme Review. Clean Break archive, Bishopsgate, London.

Clean Break (n.d.) 'About Us', www.cleanbreak.org.uk/about/. [accessed 3 December 2022].

Clean Break (n.d.) 'Short Courses and Progression Routes', https://cleanbreak.org.uk/narrative/. [accessed 20 January 2023].

Clean Break (2011) 'Clean Break Student Prospectus 2011–12', Clean Break archive, Bishopsgate, London.

Clean Break (2015) 'Clean Break Student Prospectus 2014–15', Clean Break archive, Bishopsgate, London.

Clean Break (2018) 'New Model Press Release', Clean Break archive, Bishopsgate, London.

Cooper, Mary (2008) *Missing*. Unpublished play text, Clean Break archives, Bishopsgate, London.

Corston, Jean (2007) *The Corston Report: A Report by Baroness Jean Corston of a Review of Women with Particular Vulnerabilities in the Criminal Justice System*, London: Crown Copyright.

Covington, Stephanie (2014) 'Creating Gender-Responsive and Trauma-Informed Services for Women in the Justice System', *Magistrate*. The Magistrates' Association: London. October/November, 70.5, 2–3. www.stephaniecovington.com/site/assets/files/1522/magistrate-october-november-2014-scs-interview-low-res.pdf.

Crewe, Ben et al. (2013) 'The Emotional Geography of Prison Life', *Theoretical Criminology*, 18.1, 56–74.

Craig, Sandy (ed.) (1980) *Dreams and Deconstructions: Alternative Theatre in Britain*, Ambergate: Amber Lane Press.

Daniels, Sarah (1994) *Sarah Daniels: Plays Two*, London: Bloomsbury.

Devlin, Angela (1998) *Invisible Women: What's Wrong with Women's Prisons?*, United Kingdom: Waterside.

DiCenzo, Maria (1996) *The Politics of Alternative Theatre in Britain, 1968–1990: The Case of 7:84 (Scotland)*, Cambridge: Cambridge University Press.

Drinkwater, Nicola and Davey, Kate (2017) *Clinks and National Criminal Justice Arts Alliance Case Study: Clean Break*. https://artsincriminaljustice.org.uk/wp-content/uploads/2016/07/Clean-Break-case-study-August-2017.pdf. [accessed 1 March 2023].

Duakas, Nancy (2019) 'Epistemic Justice and Injustice' in Miranda Fricker, Peter J. Graham, David Henderson, and Nikolaj J. L. L. Henderson (eds.), *The Routledge Companion of Social Epistemology*, Abingdon: Routledge, 327–334.

Efemera (1978) Original Programme for Ask'Em Out, Clean Break archive, Bishopsgate, London.

Fair, Helen and Walmsley, Roy (2021) 'World Prison Population List. Thirteenth Edition', London: Institute for Criminal Policy Research.

Foucault, Michel (1977) *Discipline and Punish: The Birth of the Prison*, London: Penguin.

Franzmann, Vivienne (2015) *Sounds Like an Insult*, unpublished play text, London: Clean Break.

Franzmann, Vivienne (2014) *Pests*, London: Nick Hern Books.

Fricker, Miranda (2007) *Epistemic Injustice: Power & the Ethics of Knowing*, Oxford: Oxford University Press.

Fricker, Miranda (2010) *Epistemic Injustice: Power and the Ethics of Knowing*, Oxford: University of Oxford Press.

Fricker, Miranda (2016) 'Epistemic Injustice and the Preservation of Ignorance', in P. Rik and B. Martijn (eds.) *The Epistemic Dimensions of Ignorance*, Cambridge: Cambridge University Press, 144–59.

Fricker, Miranda, Graham, Peter J., Henderson, David and Henderson, Nikolaj J. L. L. (2019) *The Routledge Companion of Social Epistemology*, Abingdon: Routledge.

Garland, David (1990) *Punishment and Modern Society: A Study of Social Theory*, New York: Oxford University Press.

Godard, John (2013) 'Labour Law and Union Recognition in Canada: A Historical Institutionalist Perspective', *Queen's Law Journal*, 38.2, 391–417.

Goddard, Lynette (2002) 'Black Theatre Co-operative' in A. Donnell (ed.), *Companion to Contemporary Black British Culture*. Abingdon: Routledge, 48–49.

Goldman, Alvin (2019) 'The What, Why, and How of Social Epistemology' in Miranda Fricker, , P. Graham, D. Henderson and N. Henderson (eds.), *The Routledge Companion of Social Epistemology*, Abingdon and New York: Routledge, 10–20.

Goodman, Lizbeth (1993) *Contemporary Feminist Theatres: To Each Her Own*. Abingdon: Routledge.

Gregg, Stacey, Pearson, Deborah and Edkins, Lucy et al. (2019). *Inside Bitch*, London: Oberon.

Gupta, Tanika (2002) *Inside Out*, London: Oberon.

Harker, Margaret (1979) Women with the Answers. *The Evening News*. 30 August, Clean Break archive, Bishopsgate, London.

Hayle, Sonya (2012) *Hours 'til Midnight*. Unpublished play text, Clean Break archives, Bishopsgate, London.

Hayward, Keith J. (2012) 'Five Spaces of Cultural Criminology', *The British Journal of Criminology*, 52.3, 441–462.

Herrmann, Anna (2013) '"The Mothership": Sustainability and Transformation in the Work of Clean Break', in Tim Prentki and Sheila Preston (eds.), *The Applied Theatre Reader*, United Kingdom: Taylor & Francis, 328–346.

Hicks, Jenny and Boyle, Sarah (1983) 'Like Living in a Submarine', *The Abolitionist*. Radical Alternatives to Prison, 15.3. n.p.

Hicks, Jenny (2019) Conversation with Clean Break Members. London, 17 July.

Hicks, Jenny and Holborough, Jacqueline (2020) Interview with Clean Break archive project and Women Theatre Justice research team. London, 3 January.

Hicks, Jenny and Holborough, Jacqueline (1979) Personal letter to Susan McCormick, 2 April, Clean Break archive, Bishopsgate, London.

Hicks, Jenny and Holborough, Jacqueline (2018) Interview with Caoimhe McAvinchey. London, 18 December.

Hiley, Jim (1979) Inside Story. *The Observer*, Clean Break archive, Bishopsgate, London.

Hims, Katy (2013) *Billy the Girl*, London: Bloomsbury.

HM Chief Inspector of Prisons (2004) *Report on an Unannounced Inspection of HMP Durham 5–9 January 2004*, London: Home Office.

Holborough, Jacqueline (1979a) Personal letter to Susan McCormick, 3 May, Clean Break archive, Bishopsgate, London.

Holborough, Jacqueline (1979b) Personal letter to Susan McCormick, 19 July, Clean Break archive, Bishopsgate, London.

Holborough, Jacqueline (1979c) Personal letter to Susan McCormick, 13 August, Clean Break archive, Bishopsgate, London.

Holborough, Jacqueline (1979d) Personal letter to Susan McCormick, 25 September, Clean Break archive, Bishopsgate, London.

Holborough, Jacqueline (1980) *Killers,* unpublished play text, Clean Break archive, Bishopsgate, London.

Holborough, Jacqueline (1980a) Personal letter to Susan McCormick, 10 March, Clean Break archive, Bishopsgate, London.

Holborough, Jacqueline (1980b) Personal letter to Susan McCormick, 8 May, Clean Break archive, Bishopsgate, London.

Holborough, Jacqueline (1980c) Personal letter to Susan McCormick, 23 June, Clean Break archive, Bishopsgate, London.

Holborough, Jacqueline (1981) 'An experience that should not be missed'. *The Observer*. 29 November, Clean Break archive, Bishopsgate, London.

Holborough, Jacqueline (1984) *Decade*, unpublished play text, Clean Break archive, Bishopsgate, London.

Holborough, Jacqueline (2013) Interview with Susan Croft, *Unfinished Histories*, London. www.unfinishedhistories.com/history/companies/clean-break/.

Holborough, Jaqueline, Needs, Caroline and Tilley, Alison (1981) *Avenues*, unpublished play text, Clean Break archive, Bishopsgate, London.

Itzin, Catherine (ed.) (1983) *British Alternative Theatre Directory of Playwrights, Directors and Designers*, London: John Offord.

Jeffers, Alison and Moriarty, Gerri (2017) *Culture, Democracy and the Right to Make Art: The British Community Arts Movement*. London: Bloomsbury.

Jones, Moya (2021) 'Alternative Theatre in Britain in the Late 70s and in the 80s', *Revue Française de Civilisation Britannique / French Journal of British Studies*, 'Aspects of the Underground and Mainstream in British and Irish Cultural Production since 1979', XXVI–3, 1–13.

Joseph, Jennifer (2019) *Inside Bitch*. Post-show discussion at the Royal Court Theatre, 12 March, London.

Kennedy, Helena (1993) *Eve Was Framed: Women and British Justice*, London: Vintage.

Kennedy, Helena (2018) *Eve Was Shamed: How British Justice Is Failing Women*, London: Chatto and Windus.

Kirkwood, Lucy (2008) *Cakehole*. Unpublished play text, Clean Break archives, Bishopsgate, London.

Kirkwood, Lucy (2009) *It Felt Empty When the Heart Went at First but It's Alright Now*, London: Nick Hern Books.

Lavery, Bryony (1991) *Wicked*, London: Methuen.

Lombroso, Caesar and Ferrero, William (1895) *The Female Offender*, London: T. Fisher Unwin.

NCP (2011) *Unlocking Value: The Economic Benefit of the Arts in Criminal Justice*, London: New Philanthropy Capital.

LT (1981) Review of *Avenues*. Edinburgh Evening News, 20 August, Clean Break archive, Bishopsgate, London.

McAvinchey, Caoimhe (2020) *Applied Theatre: Women and the Criminal Justice System*, London: Bloomsbury.

McCorkel, Jill (2013) *Breaking Women: Gender, Race and the New Politics of Imprisonment*, New York: New York University Press.

McIvor, Gill (ed.) (2004) *Women Who Offend*, London: Jessica Kingsley.

Merrill, E. and S. Frigon (2015) 'Performative Criminology and the "State of Play" for Theatre with Criminalized Women', *Societies*, 5(2): 1–19.

Moore, Linda and Scranton, Phil (2014) *The Incarceration of Women: Punishing Bodies, Breaking Spirits*, Basingstoke: Palgrave Macmillan.

Moran, Dominique, Turner, Jennifer and Anna K. Schliehe (2018) 'Conceptualizing the Carceral in Carceral Geography', *Progress in Human Geography*, 42.5, 666–686.

Morrison, Lucy (2020) Interview with Clean Break archive project and Women Theatre Justice research team. London, 10 February.

Moss, Chloë (2008) *This Wide Night*, London: Nick Hern Books.

Moss, Chloë (2017) *Sweatbox*, unpublished text, London: Clean Break archive.

Moss, Chloë (2015) *Sweatbox*. Unpublished play text, Clean Break archives, Bishopsgate, London.

Mottley, Eva and Hicks, Jennifer (1980) *In or Out?*, unpublished play text, Clean Break archives, Bishopsgate, London.

Mountbatten, Lord of Burma (1966) *Report of the Inquiry into Prison Escapes and Security*, London: HMSO.

'Panto in a Prison' (1978) *Yorkshire Evening Post,* 1 February, Clean Break archive, Bishopsgate, London.

Penal Reform International (2021) *Global Prison Trends*, London: Penal Reform International. https://cdn.penalreform.org/wp-content/uploads/2021/05/Global-prison-trends-2021.pdf [accessed 10 June 2022].

Pohlhaus, Gaile (2012) 'Relational Knowing and Epistemic Injustice: Toward a Theory of Willful Hermeneutical Ignorance', *Hypatia*, 27.3, 715–735.

Povinelli, Elizabeth. A. (2011) *Economies of Abandonment: Social Belonging and Endurance in Late Liberalism*. United Kingdom: Duke University Press.

Palmer, Martyn and Forlong, James (1980) 'Inside Look at Arts Behind Bars', Newspaper unknown. Exact date unknown, Clean Break archive, Bishopsgate, London.

Perman, Lucy (2019) Unpublished Interview with Caoimhe McAvinchey. London, 1 August.

Phoenix, Jo (2012) 'Book Review Symposium: Pat Carlen, *A Criminological Imagination: Essays on Justice, Punishment and Discourse*', *Punishment & Society*, 14.2, 247–26.

Pinnock, Winsome (1996) *Mules*, London: Faber and Faber.

Pinnock, Winsome (2011) *Cleaning Up*. Unpublished play text, Clean Break archives, Bishopsgate, London.

Owers, Anne (2006) 'Women in Prison', *HMP Inspectorate of Prisons*, United Kingdom.

Rafter, Nicole and Brown, Michelle (2011) *Criminology Goes to the Movies: Crime Theory and Popular Culture*, New York: New York University Press.

Ramsbotham, David (1997) *Women in Prison: A Thematic Review by Her Majesty's Chief Inspector of Prisons*. London: Home Office.

Randall, Paulette (1991) *24%*, unpublished play text, Clean Break archives, Bishopsgate, London.

Razia, Ambreen (2022) *Favour*. London: Nick Hern Books.

Rickford, Frankie (1979) 'Voices from Jail for Festival'. Newspaper unknown, 9 June 1979. Clean Break archive, Bishopsgate, London.

Ross, Raymond (1981) *Review of Avenues: The Scotsman*, Clean Break archive, Bishopsgate, London.

Routley, Laura (2017) *The Carceral: Beyond, around, through and within Prison Walls*, Political Geography, 57, 102–105.

Randall, Paulette (2020) Interview with Clean Break archive project and Women Theatre Justice research team. London, 21 February.

Reid, Julian (2022) 'On Endurance', in N. Salazar, J. Scheerder, (eds.), *Contemporary Meanings of Endurance: An Interdisciplinary Approach*, London: Routledge.

Rebellato, Dan (1999) *1956 and All That: The Making of Modern British Drama*, London: Routledge.

Rebellato, Dan (2013) *Modern British Playwrighting 2000–2009: Voices, Documents, New Interpretations*, London: Methuen Drama.

Saunders, Graham (2015) *British Theatre Companies: 1980–1994: Joint Stock, Gay Sweatshop, Complicite, Forced Entertainment, Women's Theatre Group, Talawa*, London: Bloomsbury.

Seaton, Somalia (2016) *House*, London: Nick Hern Books.

Shalson, Lara (2018) *Performing Endurance: Art and Politics Since 1960*, Cambridge: Cambridge University Press, 2018.

Sharpe, Gilly (2012) *Offending Girls: Young Women and Youth Justice*, Abingdon: Routledge.

Shellard, Dominic (1999) *British Theatre Since the War*. New Haven: Yale University Press.

Stern, Vivien (1998) *A Sin against the Future: Imprisonment in the World*, Boston, MA: Northeastern University.

Thelen, Kathleen (2010) 'Beyond Comparative Statics: Historical Institutional Approaches to Stability and Change in the Political Economy of Labor', in Glenn Morgan, John L. Campbell, Colin Crouch, Ove K. Pedersen and Richard Whitley (eds.), *The Oxford Handbook of Comparative Institutional Analysis*, Oxford: Oxford University Press, 42–62.

UK Parliament (2020) 'Statement on Reforms to Probation Services in England and Wales', www.parliament.uk/ [accessed 10 April 2023].

Velada Billson, Vishni (2020) Interview with Clean Break archive project and Women Theatre Justice research team. London, 31 January.

Wacquant, Loïc (2011) *Deadly Symbiosis: Race and the Rise of the Penal State*, Cambridge: Polity Press.

Walsh, Aylwyn (2019) *Prison Cultures: Performance, Resistance, Desire*, United Kingdom: Intellect Books.

Wandor, Michelene (1984) 'The Impact of Feminism on the Theatre', *Feminist Review*, 18, Cultural Politics, 76–92.

Wandor, Michelene (1986) *Carry on Understudies: Theatre and Sexual Politics*, London: Routledge.

Yancey Martin, Patricia (1990) 'Rethinking Feminist Organizations', *Gender & Society*, 4.2, 182–206.

Zerubavel, Eviatar (2003) *Time Maps: Collective Memory and the Social Shape of the Past*, Chicago: University of Chicago Press.

Zerubavel, Eviatar (1993) 'In the Beginning: Notes soon the Social Construction of Historical Discontinuity', *Sociological Inquiry*, 63.4, 457–459.

Funding Statement

The research for this book was carried out as part of the Arts and Humanities Research Council (AHRC) funded project, 'Clean Break: Women, Theatre, Organisation and the Criminal Justice System (2019–2023)'. The authors would like to thank Clean Break for their generous collaboration, facilitating unprecedented access to the company's work and engaging in rich conversations that have shaped our understanding of its work in context. More information about this project, including a range of publications, films and artworks made in response to it, can be found at the Women/Theatre/Justice website: https://womentheatrejustice.org/

Cambridge Elements

Women Theatre Makers

Elaine Aston
Lancaster University

Elaine Aston is internationally acclaimed for her feminism and theatre research. Her monographs include *Caryl Churchill* (1997); *Feminism and Theatre* (1995); *Feminist Theatre Practice* (1999); *Feminist Views on the English Stage* (2003); and *Restaging Feminisms* (2020). She has served as Senior Editor of Theatre Research International (2010–12) and President of the International Federation for Theatre Research (2019–23).

Melissa Sihra
Trinity College Dublin

Melissa Sihra is Associate Professor in Drama and Theatre Studies at Trinity College Dublin. She is author of *Marina Carr: Pastures of the Unknown* (2018) and editor of *Women in Irish Drama: A Century of Authorship and Representation* (2007). She was President of the Irish Society for Theatre Research (2011–15) and is currently researching a feminist historiography of the Irish playwright and co-founder of the Abbey Theatre, Lady Augusta Gregory.

Advisory Board

Nobuko Anan, *Kansai University, Japan*
Awo Mana Asiedu, *University of Ghana*
Ana Bernstein, *UNIRIO, Brazil*
Elin Diamond, *Rutgers, USA*
Bishnupriya Dutt, *JNU, India*
Penny Farfan, *University of Calgary, Canada*
Lesley Ferris, *Ohio State University, USA*
Lisa FitzPatrick, *University of Ulster, Northern Ireland*
Lynette Goddard, *Royal Holloway, University of London, UK*
Sarah Gorman, *Roehampton University, UK*
Aoife Monks, *Queen Mary, London University, UK*
Kim Solga, *Western University, Canada*
Denise Varney, *University of Melbourne, Australia*

About the Series

This innovative, inclusive series showcases women-identifying theatre makers from around the world. Expansive in chronological and geographical scope, the series encompasses practitioners from the late nineteenth century onwards and addresses a global, comprehensive range of creatives – from playwrights and performers to directors and designers.

Cambridge Elements⁼

Women Theatre Makers

Elements in the Series

Maya Rao and Indian Feminist Theatre
Bishnupriya Dutt

Xin Fengxia and the Transformation of China's Ping Opera
Siyuan Liu

Emma Rice's Feminist Acts of Love
Lisa Peck

Women Making Shakespeare in the Twenty-First Century
Kim Solga

Clean Break Theatre Company
Caoimhe McAvinchey, Sarah Bartley, Deborah Dean and Anne-marie Greene

A full series listing is available at: www.cambridge.org/EWTM

For EU product safety concerns, contact us at Calle de José Abascal, 56–1°, 28003 Madrid, Spain or eugpsr@cambridge.org.

www.ingramcontent.com/pod-product-compliance
Lightning Source LLC
LaVergne TN
LVHW020351260326
834688LV00045B/1655